THE GREATEST BOOKS OF ANCIENT INDIA

Prof. (Dr.) R. Thiagarajan started his career as a teacher and went on to become Reader and Head, Department of Sanskrit, Presidency College, Chennai, teaching Sanskrit and allied cultural subjects there for over 30 years. He has authored many audio and print books in Tamil, Sanskrit and English, besides translations and textbooks for schools and colleges. He is the founder of the Fellowship of Sanskrit Culture and has been awarded twice by the governor of Tamil Nadu for his contributions to Sanskrit. He is the chairman of Swami Dayananda's Digital Library and Research Centre, Chennai, and the chairperson of the Sanskrit Text Book Committee, Government of Tamil Nadu.

Dr. Pradeep Chakravarthy graduated from the London School of Economics, UK, and JNU, Delhi. He has a PhD in history. His corporate career at TVS, Cognizant, Infosys and McKinsey helps him connect history to human behaviour. He has authored 12 books for adults, and published several articles in magazines and newspapers on history and its relevance today. He has started 'Anantya in the Village', a heritage hotel close to one of India's oldest villages where he organizes summer workshops for children. His first book for young readers, *The History of South India for Children*, was published by Hachette India in 2024.

THE GREATEST BOOKS OF ANCIENT INDIA

INCREDIBLE IDEAS ABOUT SCIENCE, MUSIC, MATHS, ART AND MORE

hachette
INDIA

First published in paperback in 2026 by Hachette India
(Registered name: Hachette Book Publishing India Pvt. Ltd)
An Hachette UK company
www.hachetteindia.com

1

ISBN 978-93-5731-396-4

Hachette Book Publishing India Pvt. Ltd
4th & 5th Floors, Corporate Centre
Plot No. 94, Sector 44, Gurugram – 122003, India

Typeset by Manmohan Kumar, Delhi

Printed and bound in India
by Manipal Technologies Limited

FSC www.fsc.org
MIX
Paper | Supporting responsible forestry
FSC™ C043100

Every book begins with a voice.
Every voice begins with a story.
This book is dedicated to all those who
have kept the language and knowledge alive,
threading it through generations like a sacred flame.
And to those yet to come, who will learn it
and use it to shape this world
into a place of greater beauty.

CONTENTS

WHAT IS THIS BOOK ABOUT?

Did you know that some of the oldest books in the world are packed with science, maths and big questions about life? Hidden in Sanskrit texts – hundreds and thousands of years old – are secrets about the earth and sky, the human mind, nature, everyday life and how people long ago understood the world. If you're curious about what they knew and thought about subjects ranging from mathematics to astronomy, medicine to environmental studies and more – this book is for you! It's a fascinating introduction to 14 important works written in ancient India – all in Sanskrit! It offers a snapshot of each book, giving you a sneak peek into their brilliant ideas.

But what kinds of books made it into this collection?

- They were all written in Sanskrit.
- They come from different parts of India.
- They are non-fiction (so no stories or poems!).

- Each one is considered to be the best book in Sanskrit on the subject.
- The books are at least 250 years old – and most are much older than that!

  Some of these texts belong to the early medieval period. However, they were composed in Sanskrit and are part of pre-modern Indian knowledge systems, so they can be collectively considered as ancient Indian texts, along with the older texts.

Starting from the next chapter, you'll find a section on each book, arranged by subject. But there's no set order – feel free to skip around and explore the ones that interest you most!

Before diving into the books themselves, it's helpful to understand a bit about Sanskrit – what it is, where it came from and why it's so important.

SANSKRIT'S SECRETS

India is home to 22 officially recognized major languages. Of these, all – except Tamil – are either derived from or closely related to Sanskrit. Some people call Sanskrit a 'dead language' because few speak it in daily life. But that's wrong – Sanskrit is very much alive through the many Indian languages it continues to influence.

In fact, if you look closely, the names of many of the people you know are probably Sanskrit in origin. Even languages like Tamil, which belong to a different language family (Dravidian), still contain many Sanskrit words.

Sanskrit's influence doesn't stop at India's borders. To the east, countries like Cambodia (from the Sanskrit word

'Kambuja') and Indonesia show its reach. The Indonesian language, Bahasa Indonesia, has many Sanskrit-derived words. 'Bahasa' itself comes from the Sanskrit word 'bhAshA', meaning 'language'.

To the west, Sanskrit is related to ancient languages such as Latin, Greek, Avestan (of ancient Iran) and Lithuanian. These connections trace back to the larger Indo-European language family, showing just how far Sanskrit's roots stretch.

Be a Word Detective!

Find out the meanings of the names of your family members, friends, or even your own name. How many of them have Sanskrit roots?

HOW OLD IS SANSKRIT, REALLY?

Once, the legend goes, Lord Shiva danced for his favourite sages. From his damaru (a small drum in his right hand) came all the phonemes – all the basic sounds our vocal cords can make through our mouths. These 14 sets of sounds are called the Shiva Sutras, and from them, they say, came the Sanskrit language. The Sanskrit alphabet popped into existence from phonemes (the smallest unit of sound in a language), such as अ (a), इ (i), ह (h) and so on.

Linguists – those clever people who study languages – believe that thousands of years ago, a common ancestral language was spoken in the region between modern-day

Europe and Asia. This ancient tongue, known as Proto-Indo-European, existed around 5,000 years ago. The most accepted view is that Sanskrit emerged as one of the languages from the eastern branch of this Indo-European family around 1500 BCE (roughly 3,500 years ago), although another group of scholars believes that Sanskrit originated in the subcontinent itself. We don't know the right answer! Maybe it was a bit of both!

Whatever the views, the language evolved – shaped by geography, time and contact with local cultures – and began to develop grammar, vocabulary and structure. At this stage, there was still no writing – just speech passed down through the generations.

Around 1000 BCE – roughly 3,000 years ago – ancient Sanskrit religious hymns and verses were compiled into what became known as the Rig Veda, the earliest known Sanskrit text. For centuries, it was transmitted by word of mouth using strict oral traditions, which ensured that every syllable and accent remained intact. It wasn't written down until much later.

ENTER PANINI – THE SOUND ORGANIZER

Have you ever been told to 'put everything back in its proper place' or to 'tidy up that mess'? Grown-ups can be very particular about keeping books stacked, chairs straight and shoes lined up. It may feel like a bit of a pain – but eventually you'll see how useful a little organizing can be.

One example of that is Panini, a brilliant mind from around the fifth century BCE – more than 2,000 years ago! While we don't know much about him, his work has lasted through the ages. He wrote an extraordinary book called

A STAMP COMMEMORATING PANINI

the *Ashtadhyayi* – which means 'Book of Eight Chapters'. It's not a storybook, but a highly detailed grammar guide that brought order to the Sanskrit language like never before.

One of Panini's greatest contributions is the way he organized the alphabet. Instead of keeping it all jumbled up (like the English ABCs!), he arranged it logically, like a perfect filing system for sounds:

- **Swaras – the vowels**: These are the 'singing' sounds, or the ones you can say with parted lips – like aaa or ooo. They can stand alone and flow freely.
- **Consonants – the grouped sounds**: These need help from vowels to be fully pronounced. Panini didn't just lump them together – he organized them based on:
  - where the sound is made in the mouth (throat, tongue, lips, and so on).
  - how much effort it takes to produce the sound (a light or heavy touch of the tongue).
  - for how long the sound can be held (for example, the way aaaa can stretch but ka cannot).
  - whether it stands alone or needs a vowel to sound complete.

The result?

A beautifully structured system of 48 basic sounds: 13 vowels and 35 consonants, arranged scientifically. Sanskrit learners now had a clear and practical way to understand and work with sounds. Isn't that clever? Panini basically gave us a sound 'toolbox' – where everything is labelled, sorted and easy to find. It was a masterpiece of logic and organization, far ahead of its time.

The 13 consonants were divided into five groups of five letters each. If you slowly recite each letter of the Sanskrit alphabet, you'll actually feel the brilliance of Panini's system. Panini applied rule #1 of great organization: 'Put everything in its rightful place.'

Panini didn't just write a grammar book – he gave us a scientific system for organizing sound, which is still admired by linguists around the world today.

क	ka	ख	kha	ग	ga	घ	gha	ङ	ng
च	cha	छ	chha	ज	ja	झ	jha	ञ	jna
ट	Ta	ठ	Tha	ड	Da	ढ	Dha	ण	Na
त	ta	थ	tha	द	da	ध	dha	न	na
प	pa	फ	pha	ब	ba	भ	bha	म	ma
य	ya	र	ra	ल	la	व	va		
श	sha	ष	Sha	स	sa	ह	ha		

A NEW NAME!

Panini organized Sanskrit with such precision in his *Ashtadhyayi* that it completely changed the way people saw the language, which they simply called 'BhAshA' or 'Veda BhAshA' (the language used in sacred rituals and mantras). Now, it was no longer just a language – it had become something special. Sanskrit became the classical language of ancient India and the root of many modern Indian languages.

It needed a new name!

After Panini's work, 'bhAsha' continued to be the word used for 'language' in general, but the version refined by Panini became known as 'Samskrutham' – the 'well-crafted' or 'perfected' language.

Over time, the word 'Samskrutham' became simplified in everyday speech to 'Sanskrit', which is the name we now use.

A MASTERPIECE OF RULES

Panini's *Ashtadhyayi* contains about 4,000 grammar rules, all written so clearly that they can be learnt like formulas (which is what students of Sanskrit often do)!

He also drew from an earlier text – the *Amarakosha*, a kind of dictionary or thesaurus compiled by someone called Amarasimha. Sanskrit learners still memorize this book to this day – not all at once, but bit by bit, like learning the multiplication tables. It's full of synonyms and categories of vocabulary – and it became surprisingly fun and logical with practice!

Later, a great sage named Patanjali – famous for the Yoga Sutras – wrote a commentary on Panini's grammar, called the *Mahabhashya* (literally, 'Great Commentary'), somewhat like an ancient user manual!

SANSKRIT AND PRAKRIT: TWO STYLES OF SPEAKING

After Panini, Samskrutham was mainly used by scholars, priests and in royal courts. Everyday people spoke a simpler, easy-going version of Sanskrit called PrAkrit – which means 'natural' or 'original'.

You can think of it like this: just as in our SMS and WhatsApp messages we use 'fr' instead of 'for real' or 'idk' instead of 'I don't know', people back then used casual forms (acronyms and abbreviations) in daily life and formal forms for learning, rituals or literature.

In other words, Sanskrit was formal and structured – the way you would write in the classroom – and PrAkrit was informal and natural – like texting a friend!

For example, the Sanskrit word 'dharma' became 'dhamma' in PrAkrit – easier to pronounce in everyday, casual speech. There were many different forms of PrAkrit across India, and PAli was among the most popular versions. This was the language used by Gautama Buddha to share his teachings.

And here's the fun part – PAli travelled! As Buddhism spread to Sri Lanka and South-East Asia, so did PAli. It's like the language went on a long vacation...and stayed there! You see, languages change, adapt and travel. That's what keeps them alive.

SANSKRIT BOOKS – THEN AND NOW

By the fifth century CE, Sanskrit had become the language of educated people across much of the subcontinent. While Tamil remained widely spoken and respected in the south, Sanskrit was the preferred language for education, literature, science and official communication across much of the Indian subcontinent.

Interestingly, Sanskrit didn't have its own script! It remained a spoken language for a long time. When people needed to write it down, different regions used their local scripts. In the north, these included scripts like the Brahmi, Gupta, Sharada and Nagari scripts across different time periods. In the south, it was written in Grantha, Telugu or Kannada scripts.

So, why do we use Devanagari to write Sanskrit today?

About 200 years ago, when Sanskrit books started being printed in Maharashtra, they used the Marathi script, which is very similar to Devanagari. That version gradually became the standard printed script for Sanskrit across India. So, while Sanskrit is a language, Devanagari is just the script – just as English is written using the Roman alphabet.

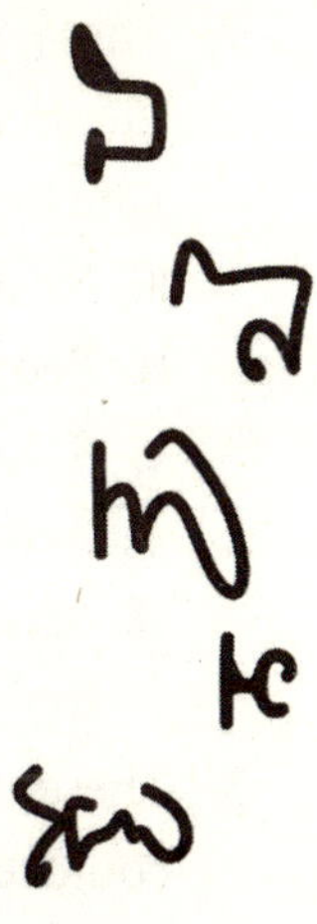

ANCIENT KNOWLEDGE IN SANSKRIT

Because Sanskrit was the language of educated people, important knowledge was recorded in Sanskrit – not just religious or philosophical texts but also books for everyday life! Some of the best minds – philosophers, scientists, poets, doctors, dramatists – thought, spoke and wrote in Sanskrit.

We'll be exploring some of these books in this book you are holding – it's like opening treasure chests of ancient wisdom!

Millions of works have been written in Sanskrit – books, plays, poems, songs, stories, science texts and much, much more. Although many have been lost, countless others remain – simply waiting to be explored. Of course, there are many such written documents (or manuscripts). In this book, we've chosen a handful of fascinating non-fiction Sanskrit texts – real works from real lives – from different parts of India and across different time periods.

Here's what you'll notice:

1. For many of these books, we don't even know who the authors were. That's right! They didn't think it was important to tell us their name or life story. Maybe they felt their work should speak for itself. Rather clever, don't you think?
2. These texts were not published like books today, with identical copies all over the world. They were handwritten, which meant:
    a. Mistakes could creep in;
    b. People could add or leave out sections;
    c. Some books survive in only one known copy, like the *Arthashastra*; and
    d. Many books are lost forever because no one bothered to make copies.
3. These precious texts were written on palm leaves, which could easily tear, wear out or rot in the rain or humid

weather. Transporting them across ancient India – without the modern means of transport we have now – was slow and risky. Therefore, the fact that any of these books have survived is nothing short of a miracle – like keeping your homework safe for thousands of years!

If these books have survived hundreds of years of rain, fire, war and time, there must be something valuable in them for us. Let's find out what! It's like stepping into a time machine – zooming back across centuries to listen to voices from the past, still alive in the words they left behind.

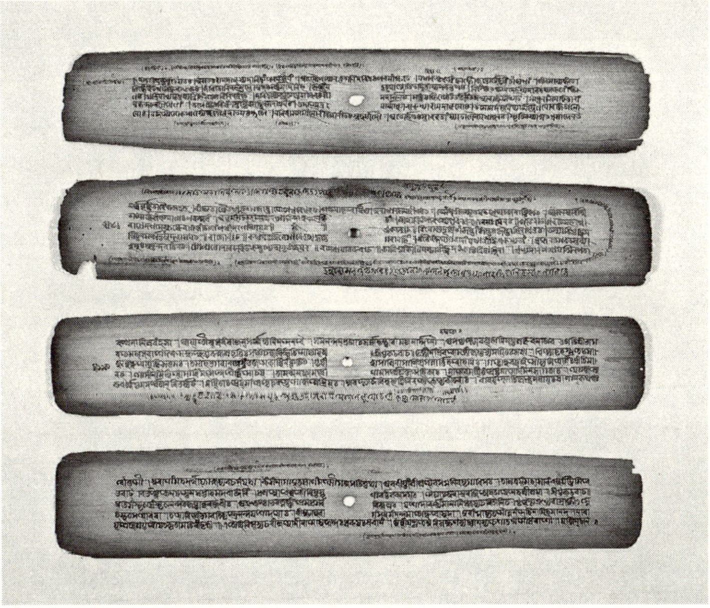

THIS IS WHAT A MANUSCRIPT ON PALM LEAVES LOOKED LIKE – PAGES FROM THE *BHAGAVATA PURANA*

1

ASTRONOMY AND MATHEMATICS

ARYABHATIYA

People in olden times were as fascinated by the night sky as everyone is today: the twinkling stars, the moon…sometimes the planets and the Milky Way!

There was also a practical aspect to studying the skies. They used it to tell time, not just the hours and minutes, but also the movement of the sun and the moon, which determined when to plant crops, and the constellations helped with navigation and guided travellers.

Imagine how, in the past, people like Aryabhata and other astronomers studied the sky using just their eyes. They described so many things about the celestial bodies.

THE BOOK

Who was Aryabhata, and what is the book about?

Aryabhata was born in 476 CE (more than 1,500 years ago) in Kusumapura, which is now identified as Patna in Bihar.

Aryabhata wrote two books: *Aryabhatiya*, which is available, and *Aryabhata Sidhanta*, which is lost.

The *Aryabhatiya* has 121 verses in Sanskrit divided into four parts:

Parts	What It's About	Verses
1 GItikA-pAda	Basic definitions and concepts	13
2 GaNita-pAda	Maths (most of it later included in another book, *Lilavati*)	33
3 KalAkriyA-pAda	Astronomy. Units and the measurement of time and how to determine the true positions of the celestial bodies	25
4 GOla-pAda	The movements of the sun, the moon and the planets	50

All the verses are very short and precise. To understand them, astronomers who came much later wrote commentaries, explaining the original verses in their own words. Even 600 years after Aryabhata died, his book was so famous that people wrote commentaries on it in present-day Jammu and Kashmir, Madhya Pradesh, Uttar Pradesh, Gujarat, Rajasthan, Maharashtra, Karnataka, Andhra Pradesh, Kerala and Tamil Nadu. Handwritten copies travelled so far and wide!

WHY IS THIS BOOK IMPORTANT?

Aryabhata discovered many things in mathematics that were rediscovered much later in Europe. Although he never claimed to have invented anything, his book lists topics that he thought were important.

In astronomy, he was the first to suggest that Earth rotated on its own axis. He discovered a simple way to explain how planets moved on their paths. He also discovered how to plot their exact positions in the sky.

Aryabhata chose a special 'standard circle' for astronomy. By setting the radius equal to 3,438 arc-minutes, the circumference of the circle closely matched the total number of arc-minutes in 360 degrees. This clever choice simplified many calculations involving angles and circular motion.

It's no wonder then that India's first satellite, built by the Indian Space Research Organization (ISRO) and launched on 19 April 1975 by the Soviet Union, was named 'Aryabhata' after this brilliant astronomer and mathematician.

INSIDE THE BOOK

Part 1 ('GItikA-pAda') has poems, most of them written in a style called the 'gItikA' metre. It explains key ideas in astronomy and has useful tables about them:

- How Aryabhata invented a system in which letters stood for numbers. In this method, consonants gave the number, and vowels showed how big that number was (ones, hundreds, thousands, millions and so on). This let him write extremely large numbers as short, easy-to-remember words. Without knowing this code, many of the 'words' in his books look meaningless, even though they're actually numbers. For example, here are some clear vowel place values:

- $a = 10^0$ (units)
- $i = 10^2$ (hundreds)
- $u = 10^4$ (ten-thousands)

    k represents 1

    u represents 10^4

    So, the syllable ku means:

    $1 \times 10{,}000 = 10{,}000$

- How they measured circles in the sky (with degrees and minutes).
- How they measured distances: Aryabhata used traditional Indian units of length such as yOjana, nr, hasta and angula. He said that the diameter of Earth at the equator (the imaginary line around the middle of Earth) was 1,050 yOjanas. Today, scientists measure Earth's diameter as 12,757 kilometres (7,927 miles). From this, we can estimate that one yOjana was about: 12½ kilometres, or 7¾ miles.

    Aryabhata also used smaller units:

    - ☐ 1 nr was about 1.5 metres (around 5 feet)
    - ☐ 1 hasta was about 1¼ feet
    - ☐ A cubitus (hasta) commonly used by people was slightly longer, about 1⅓ feet
    - ☐ The angula was a small unit, about the width of a finger
- How many times Earth and the moon and other planets go around the sun. The sidereal period is the time it takes for a celestial body like a planet to complete one revolution with respect to the fixed stars. As you can see from this table, Aryabhata was – without any fancy technology – very close to modern astronomers!

Planet	Revolutions in 43,20,000 Years	Sidereal Period in Terms of Days	
		In *Aryabhatiya*	Modern Calculations
Sun	43,20,000	365.25868	365.25636
Moon	5,77,53,336	27.32167	27.32166
Mercury	1,79,37,020	87.96988	87.96930
Venus	70,22,288	224.69814	224.70080
Mars	22,96,824	686.99974	686.97970
Jupiter	3,64,224	4332.27217	4332.58870
Saturn	1,46,564	10766.06465	10759.201

- The paths that the sun, the moon and the planets follow in the sky. They move through space along fixed paths, like invisible roads in the sky. To understand these paths, scientists imagine a flat surface, like a big sheet of paper. Earth moves around the sun on this flat surface. Other planets move on paths that are tilted, so they cross this flat surface.

  The place where a planet's path crosses upward through the flat surface is called the ascending node. It is like pushing a pencil up through a piece of paper – the point where it comes through is the ascending node. Scientists measure an angle to show where this crossing point is.

This angle is called the longitude of the ascending node. Another important point is the apogee, which is when the moon or a planet is farthest from Earth.

Aryabhata worked out all of this more than 1,500 years ago without modern tools, and his answers were very close to what scientists calculate today. (The Ptolemy mentioned below was a Greek astronomer who lived before Aryabhata.)

Longitudes of the Apogees for 499 CE

Planet	Aryabhata	Ptolemy (for 150 CE)	Modern Calculations
Sun	78°	65° 30'	77° 15'
Mars	118°	115° 30'	128° 28'
Mercury	210°	190° 00'	234° 11'
Jupiter	180°	161° 00'	170° 22'
Venus	90°	55° 00'	290° 4'
Saturn	236°	233° 00'	243° 40'

- How big Earth, the sun, the moon and the planets are.
- How tilted the orbits of the planets and the moon are when they go around the sun:

Inclinations of the Orbits

Planet	In *Aryabhatiya*	Modern Calculations
Moon	4° 30'	5° 9'
Mars	1° 30'	1° 51' 01"
Mercury	2°	7° 00' 12"

Jupiter	1°	1° 18' 28"
Venus	2°	3° 23' 38"
Saturn	2°	2° 29' 20"

- How the paths of the moon and the planets cross the sun's path.
- How the sun, moon and planets rotate and revolve.
- How to create your own sine table: Aryabhata created a list of 24 numbers used to help with certain types of calculations.

Give Me a Sine

Imagine a circle with a point moving around it. If you drop a straight vertical line down from that point, the sine tells you how high or low that point is compared to the size of the circle. It's like measuring the height of a person riding a Ferris wheel: sometimes they're high up, sometimes they're low down, and the sine tells us exactly how high or low they are.

Sine tables are used for more than circle-related calculations. When something is tilted, the word sine tells us how steep the tilt is. It compares how high something goes or how long it is. You don't need to do the hard math yourself – that's where the table comes in.

A sine table is a chart that:

- lists angles (like 0°, 30°, 45°, 60°, 90°);
- shows the sine value for each angle.

It's kind of like a multiplication table, but instead of numbers × numbers, it's angles from which you get the answers. Before calculators existed, people used sine tables to:

- measure the height of mountains, trees, ramps...
- find the distance to stars.
- build temples, bridges and ships.

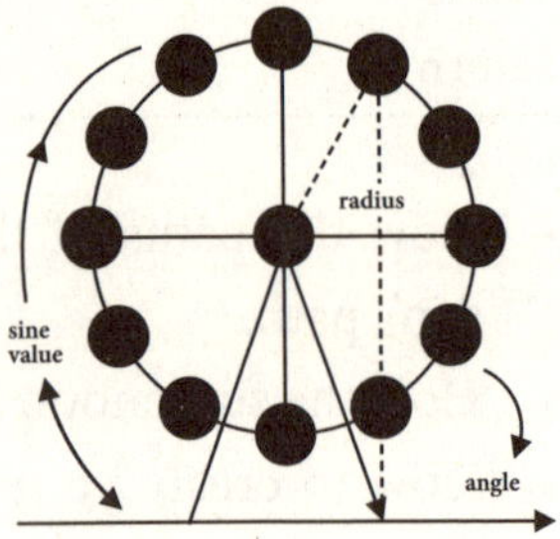

They could look at an angle, check the table, and get the number they needed. Even though sine comes from circles, sine tables are mostly used to work with triangles (especially right-angled triangles), slopes and heights and distances you can't measure directly.

Instead of writing down the sine values themselves (as we do today), Aryabhata wrote the differences between one value and the next. This made the table shorter and easier to use at the time. This clever method helped ancient astronomers calculate angles and work out the positions of stars and planets long before calculators or computers existed. Sine tables were also used to build bridges, measure mountains, navigate ships and, yes, solve math problems in school!

Part 2 ('GaNita-pAda') is all about mathematics. If Part 1 was about astronomy measurements, this is like a maths book!

Much of this is in the *Lilavati* (see chapter 7 of the book), so we'll move on to the astronomy stuff in later chapters. But briefly, this chapter explains:

- How to measure the areas of triangles, circles and trapeziums, as well as the volume of tetrahedrons and spheres.

- How to solve problems about shadows cast by a gnomon (like a sundial stick).
- Math problems in a series (number patterns).
- How to calculate interest (like when you put money in a bank account).
- Special mathematics tricks like finding square roots, cube roots and creating a sine table.

Share Your Discoveries

Draw your favourite constellation, write down what you find out about it, or take photos of your observations.

Ancient astronomers like Aryabhata changed the world by carefully watching the sky night after night. Who knows... perhaps YOU'LL discover something astounding too!

Remember: The same stars Aryabhata watched 1,500 years ago are still shining above you tonight. When you look up at the night sky, you're connecting with thousands of years of curious minds who wondered about the universe – just like you.

Happy stargazing!

Part 3 (called KalakriyA-pAda) has 25 poems – or stanzas – all about time and finding the real positions of the sun, the moon and the planets in the sky.

This chapter explains:

- Different ways to measure time (like months, days and so on).

Here are his rules in a tidy table:

The Time Divisions

1 year	= 12 months
1 month	= 30 days
1 day	= 60 nADIs (or nADIkAs)
1 nADI (nADIkA)	= 60 vinADIkAs
1 sidereal vinADIkA	= 60 long syallables *or*
	= 6 respirations (prANas)

The Circular Divisions

1 revolution	= 12 signs
1 sign	= 30 degrees
1 degree	= 60 minutes (kalAs)
1 minute	= 60 seconds (vikalAs)
1 second	= 60 thirds (tatparAs)

He talks about synodic periods and synodic revolutions. A synodic period is the time it takes for a planet to line up in the same way again in relation to the sun and Earth. Think of it like this: Imagine you and a friend jogging around a track at different speeds. You start side by side, then move apart. A synodic period is

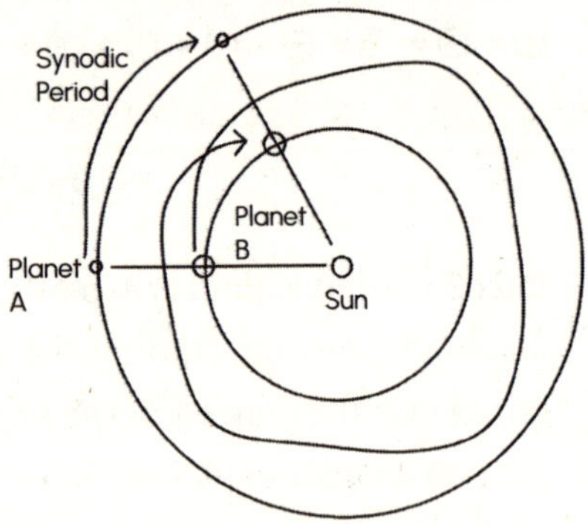

FIGURING OUT A SYNODIC PERIOD

the time it takes until you are side by side again, even though you've both been moving the whole time.

Planets do the same thing as they move around the sun at different speeds. In space, it's the time until Earth and another planet line up with the sun again. A synodic revolution is just another way of saying 'one complete synodic period'. It's the full cycle from one alignment to the next. For this, Aryabhata's calculations are startlingly close to modern calculations!

	Synodic Revolutions		
Planet	Synodic Period in Days		
	Aryabhata	Ptolemy	Modern
Moon	29.53058	29.53059	29.53059
Mars	779.92125	779.9428	779.936
Mercury	I15.8783	115.8786	115.877
Jupiter	398.8895	398.8864	398.884
Venus	583.8975	584.0000	583.921
Saturn	378.0859	378.0930	378.092

- He also measures solar and lunar years. Using this and many other calculations, we can solve a riddle he gives in this part. He says: 'When sixty times sixty years and three-quarter yugas (of the current yuga) had elapsed, twenty-three years had then passed since my birth.'

  This means 3,600 years had elapsed since the beginning of the current Kaliyuga.

  3,600 years = 1,57,79,17,500 ÷ 1,200 or 13,14,931.25 days (he provides this formula in another verse).

The answer is the date corresponding to Sunday, 21 March 499 CE. On this day, he celebrated his 23rd birthday, which means that he was born on 21 March 476 CE.

- Many verses are about the movement and path of the sun, the moon and the planets. He says they move in special off-centre circles (called epicycles – manda vritta) and in smaller circles while going around bigger circles (called orbital circles – kakshyA vritta). He provides many detailed calculations to determine the true longitudes (positions) of the sun, the moon and the planets. This was very useful for sailors, farmers and making a calendar.

Think of this chapter as a guide to understanding how time works and how to track where things are in the sky at any given moment.

⊕•⊕•⊕

Part 4 ('GOla-pAda') is the longest chapter.

The GOla (which means sphere) is like a special toy that ancient Indian astronomers built using bendy, wooden sticks or bamboo to show how the sun, the moon and the planets move across the sky. Imagine making circles with sticks and connecting them together to create a big sphere – that's what a 'gOla' is! The special type called bhagOla (meaning 'sphere of the asterisms') is designed as if Earth is in the middle of everything, and it helps people understand how stars and planets seem to travel around us in the night sky.

This chapter is all about the celestial sphere – that big imaginary ball in the sky where the stars and planets seem

A REIMAGINED BHAGOLA

to sit. It also explains how the sun, the moon and the planets move across the celestial sphere. Aryabhata made many clever calculations to map the paths they take and how these paths intersect.

- Indian astronomers thought that all the heavenly bodies – the planets, the moon and the stars – got their light from the sun. Aryabhata placed Earth at the centre with the sun and the planets orbiting around it. We now know that not all these ideas are true, but they made sense for his time since he studied the skies only with his eyes – and not modern telescopes. Yet, he guessed correctly that Earth spins and travels around the sun.
- Aryabhata described Earth as having an incredibly tall mountain, Mount Meru, that shone brightly. Some modern astronomers wonder if he meant the glowing aurora borealis – those dancing lights in the polar sky.

- He gave many calculations about the equator's length and the 'four cities on its corners'. He also claimed that the devas lived in the northern hemisphere while the rAkshasas lived in the southern one, where there was mostly water.
- He explained how to calculate solar and lunar eclipses, and described their various stages.

Think of this chapter as explaining how the whole 'sky machine' works together and how it looks different depending on where you are on Earth. It also teaches how to predict special events like eclipses and when you can see different planets in the sky.

He ends with a prayer to Brahma – similar to one he started with – and says that whatever he has written will hold true for all time. Some of it did turn out to be!

A big thanks to Prof. R. Gopu for his feedback on this chapter. To know more, visit https://varahamihiragopu.blogspot.com/

2

ARCHITECTURE

MAYAMATA

There was once a super-architect called Maya, who was so brilliant that people called him the 'Architect of the Gods'! The *Mayamata* contains all of Maya's incredible wisdom about designing and building amazing structures on Earth (and even in heaven!).

THE BOOK

Have you ever wondered how homes were built long ago? Or how entire cities were skilfully planned? And how ancient builders managed to create such massive and beautiful temples using incredibly heavy stones? The *Mayamata* has all the answers!

This book has 36 chapters with a total of 3,000 verses in Sanskrit. It teaches everything from how to choose the perfect site to build on and how to construct houses, to how to plan entire villages, create temples and even how to carve intricate statues of gods and goddesses!

The book is divided into three main parts.

Parts	What It's About
Chapters 1–10	Finding the perfect building site because land is considered the first vAstu or object.
Chapters 11–30	Information about different types of buildings, from simple houses to grand palaces, strong forts and magnificent temples. Buildings are the second vAstu.
Chapters 31–36	The third vAstu, such as carriages, carts, palanquins, ornate chairs, royal beds and thrones. This part of the *Mayamata* also includes all the clever mathematics and science behind construction.

WHO WROTE THIS BOOK?

The origin of this text is again a mystery! We have no specific author's name. However, we do know that it was written in south India, probably in Tamil Nadu, between the 11th and 13th centuries. Back then, the powerful Chola kings were building monumental multi-storeyed temples in places like Thanjavur and Gangaikonda Cholapuram.

The book mainly talks about temples for Lord Shiva, but it also includes information about temples for Lord Vishnu, the Buddha and the Jain faith. The Chola kings supported all these religions. The *Mayamata* mentions that some Vishnu temples have two upper floors, something that another book called the *Marichi Samhita* discusses in great detail. You can see these rare multi-level temples in places like Kanchipuram,

Mannarkovil, Cheranmahadevi and Thirukoshtiyur – all in Tamil Nadu.

Over time, people have added new sections to the original text, as often happened with ancient manuscripts that were handwritten. Each person who copied it might have added their own wisdom or ideas. In Kerala, for example, their version has extra information on wooden structures because most of their buildings were made of wood rather than stone due to the rainy weather.

INSIDE THE BOOK

The *Mayamata* is a handbook on architecture, from long ago, describing how to plan cities, build houses and temples, and shape spaces where people could live, work and worship.

Part 1: It's All about the Land

You may wonder why so many chapters focus on choosing the ideal site and preparing the land for construction. Today, we often change the environment to suit our needs: mowing down forests, levelling mountains or filling lakes to create cities. But in ancient India, people held Nature sacred and wouldn't have dared to mistreat the environment. Land was called *kshetra* – a sacred place.

'The earth is our first home, and it is with her permission that any building – home or temple – can be built.' This is the first statement in the book! When choosing a site, there are special rules about the land's slope, colour, smell and even taste! Trees are also important.

- After a suitable site had been selected, they first held a ceremony to take the permission of Earth and all the living and non-living things in the space that would be affected by the building.
- A seed-sowing test proved fertility – if the seed (such as barley or sesame) sprouted, the land was considered good for farming.
- For building, there was a 'pit test'. The *Mayamata* instructs builders to dig a pit of prescribed dimensions and refill it with the excavated soil. In another variant, they would fill the pit with water and leave it overnight. If the soil fit back exactly, it was good land. If soil was left over, the land was still fine. However, if the soil was insufficient or the water drained too fast, the land would be deemed unsuitable for building.

Measurement Notes

How did people measure things in ancient times? Here's how:

- Parama aNu: so tiny that it was invisible to the naked eye. For us, 1 parama aNu ≈ 10^{-10} to 10^{-12} centimetres.
- 8 parama aNu = 1 rathareNu: a speck of dust from a chariot.
- 1 rathareNu = 6 trasareNu: tiny particles (dust motes) seen in a sunbeam.
- 1 angula (finger width): 8 barley grains placed in a row.
- 10 angulas: a hand span.

Ancient carpenters and craftsmen must've been amazing at arithmetic! Most calculations were done in their heads.

There are more measurements; we've only given you a 'parama aNu'!

The Team

Building in ancient times was as much a team effort as it is now. Here are the key people:

- **Sthapati:** The chief architect, who had to be fair in his dealings in addition to being an expert in mathematics and science.
- **SUtra grahin:** The architect's assistant, who measured everything carefully.
- **Takshaka:** The expert in cutting wood, stone or bricks.
- **Vardhaki**: The mason, who put everything together under the sUtra grahin's instructions.

In those days, people didn't have compasses! Instead, they used a *shanku* (a wooden stick) and watched the stick's shadows to figure out the direction. This process is discussed in detail in the text.

Using one square room as the basic unit, the book devises concentric square patterns of up to 1,024. The formula is 1–4–9–16… so that the building is always square-shaped. Each square has a divine being (land is sacred, remember?), and these need to be honoured with offerings, such as ghee, rice and curd – and sometimes even fish. The building is considered a human being with six lines; these are its bones. The heart is the centre square. The four vulnerable points are the four corners on the outside, and the diagonals are the arteries. The head points towards the north-east, and the feet point towards the south-west.

It Takes a Village

Chapters 9 and 10 are specifically about villages and towns. The smallest villages were 64 poles (or danda) wide, about 1,056 feet. The smallest fort was 640 poles wide. Street widths were 1, 2, 3, 4 or 5 poles wide. Streets used by the temple carts had to be wider. Locations for temples, gates, houses and shops were all mentioned. They depended on the number and patterns of the village streets. On the facing page is an example of a village where the streets are in the swastika shape. The swastika is an ancient symbol of the sun and considered very auspicious.

Part 2: Beautiful Buildings

This section explains how to design and construct houses, temples, halls, doors, pillars, roofs and decorations, along with rules for measurements, materials and artistic features that make buildings strong, useful and beautiful.

Homes were built of wood (especially their pillars) and bricks. Chapters 11–15 explain how, before laying the first bricks, a small casket with things relevant to the building's purpose or the builder must be buried in the pit. Water bodies like wells and canals are covered in these chapters.

From these chapters, we learn that houses had many windows with latticed brick or wood. They had one or more

A SWASTIKA-SHAPED LAYOUT FOR A VILLAGE – IN THE CENTRAL SQUARE WERE THE BAZAARS, AS LAID OUT BELOW

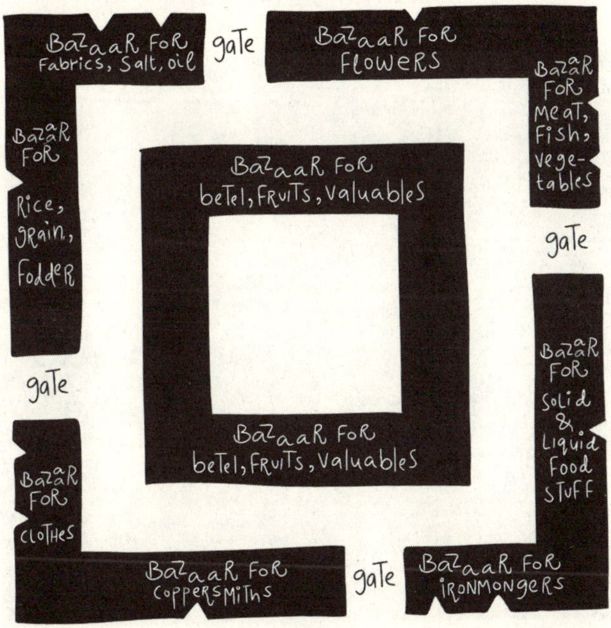

EXAMPLES OF FINIALS ON TOP OF TEMPLES (ABOVE) AND HOUSES (BELOW)

storeys connected by wooden staircases. Temples had as many as 12 storeys. The outer walls had ceiling beams that projected outwards, and the tips of these protruding beams were carved into lotus buds. Homes had attics and the roof had a finial, which was a metal or wood decorative end at the top.

The main weight of the structure was borne by the pillars. Walls were there as partitions to provide privacy. Many verses are dedicated to the way different pieces of wood need to be joined together and all the problems that could occur if this was not done carefully. A ceremony was performed when the building was complete.

Chapters 19–22 deal with the details of building stone temples with a varying number of storeys.

Chapters 23–25 deal with the building of temple walls, gateways and pillared buildings that didn't have any walls, and were therefore multipurpose. A curtain across the pillars could create a makeshift room or hall.

Chapters 26–28 deal with houses. The simplest plan was a two-roomed house that opened into a common pillared veranda. One unit of two rooms and a veranda was repeated in many ways to create more complex, larger structures, like you would with building blocks.

Buildings for monks, schools, and stables for elephants and horses are also discussed. All buildings had rooms opening into verandas and a lot of open space surrounded by rooms. The ideal combination was a courtyard surrounded by rooms on all sides, a plan common to old houses in India.

The palace was similar to the house in structure but had many more units. The text advises the king to build the palace in the centre of the town if he aspired to be powerful.

Chapter 30 is just about doors! A pair or single, where to put in the hinges, the size in connection and proportion to the lintel and so on.

Part 3: The Finer Points

This section of the *Mayamata* deals with fine details and moveable structures, such as images and sculptures, among others. It explains how these items should be measured, shaped and decorated so that they match the buildings around them.

Chapters 31–36 cover chariots, palanquins, thrones, couches and other furniture.

Three kinds of palanquins are discussed:

- with sides;
- with a simple roof; and
- with a three-layered roof.

Detailed measurements are provided, including how the wood must be cut and what joints are needed. One type of roof resembled a bald man's head.

For chariots, we have the proportions of the long beam, the crossbeams and the axle. The proportions for the pillars of the handrail are also given. Suggestions for design motifs are included.

For beds, the correct measurement is that the length must be five units and the width three units. The legs must be between 1 and 1½ hand spans and can be carved into tiger or deer legs or just kept straight.

Divans are made just like beds but can have wooden slats or straps. A divan can be suspended on chains with the hook (shaped like a crow's beak!) fixed into the roof – this is an Unjal or jhUla today!

It's best to have the head of the bed or divan to the east or west, so that the person sleeps facing south.

Squat seats on which people would sit with their legs tucked under them were built to be upholstered like beds and divans. These were square or rectangular. The legs of these seats were carved like lions, elephants, bulls or dwarves.

The lion throne, which was for kings, has more specifications, including a backrest and a lotus-shaped base.

The final chapters are about making images of gods and repairing them. The chosen stones needed to be uniformly coloured, to have a metallic ring to them and oughtn't to be damaged in any way, we are told.

Even the rituals for cutting the stone from mountains are detailed and filled with respect for the forest gods.

There are detailed notes on the size and different types of Shivalingas, depending on whether the temple is Dravida (south Indian, except Kerala), Nagara (north Indian) or Vesara (a combination).

For the opening of the idol's eyes (when the deity begins to 'live'), a gold chisel was used.

The last two chapters deal with renovations. The book says temples can be extended to the north and the east, using the same materials as in the original. There are detailed rules on when and how damaged sculptures of the deities may be repaired or replaced.

Put on a Pedestal

The statues of the gods are always mounted on pedestals. There are 16 types of pedestals. The proportion of the pedestal depends on the posture of the deity on it:

* **Reclining image** – the pedestal is 1/3rd the height of the sculpture.
* **Seated** – the pedestal is 1/4th the height of the sculpture.
* **Standing** – the pedestal is 1/5th the height of the sculpture.

The next time you're in a temple or museum, eyeball the statue to see if this formula has been used! The size of the entire temple is calculated based on the height of the main image.

When renovating houses or villages, the final size must not be less than the original size.

The last chapter gives detailed instructions on how the main gods and goddesses must look and where they must be installed. A fierce Narasimha, for example, must be installed in a forest cave on a hilltop or in the depths of an enemy's kingdom.

There are instructions on the outward appearance of the gods and deities as well: for example, a dancing Shiva must have his dreadlocks up in a topknot, decorated with crane feathers and a crescent moon, and wear a garland of skulls around his neck. The Buddha has to be dressed in red clothes, wear no jewellery and be seated cross-legged on a lion throne with the sacred fig tree (ashvattha) beside him.

Even the colours and weapons of the guardian images are mentioned in detail.

The text ends without any information about the author or compiler.

The Super-Glue of Eight Elements: Ashtabandhanam

There was no cement back then, but the strength of this 'binding glue' will surprise you. Many south Indian temples still standing today used this special bonding compound to fix idols on their pedestals and for joining important stone components such as joints and sockets, among other uses.

This was the ancient formula: To equal parts of wax, molasses, beeswax and bdellium, add some sarja resin (equal or double). Add pounded brick. Pour all of this into a metal vessel with an equal quantity of oil. Stir with a metal spoon and cook on a low flame until it thickens.

3

CHEMISTRY

RASARATNA-SAMUCCHAYA

Chemistry is like the secret recipe book of our world!

It explains why baking soda makes cookies rise and turn brown, how soap washes away dirt and why fireworks create those dazzling colours in the sky. Even your body is basically a chemistry lab – it turns food into energy so you can run, play and think.

Chemistry helps us make medicines that heal, and create materials that build smartphones and video games and warm winter clothes. Understanding it is like having superpowers – you can see how the whole world works, from tiny atoms to giant explosions!

But here's a surprise – people in ancient India were already working with chemistry over 800 years ago! They were real-life wizards – mixing metals, minerals and herbs to create medicines and new materials. Their discoveries still amaze modern scientists today.

THE BOOK

Long, long ago, in the 13th century, there lived a brilliant scientist named Acharya Rasa Vagbhata. His father, Simhagupta, was also a learned scholar. Vagbhata wrote a remarkable book called *Rasaratna-samucchaya*, which means 'Collection of Alchemical Gems'.

This wasn't just a dusty old textbook – it was a treasure trove of ancient chemistry secrets!

Imagine if you found a book that taught you how to turn rocks into medicine, purify metals into something so pure that they could heal people or shine like stars, and design awesome lab gadgets. That's what this book did for people centuries ago!

INSIDE THE BOOK

The *Rasaratna-samucchaya* has a whopping 3,871 verses under two main parts.

Part	What It's About
1. Chapters 1–11	How to transform metals and minerals into medicines using chemistry
2. Chapters 12–30	How to treat diseases using both herbal and metal-based remedies

We will focus on the first part – the chemistry adventure!

These 11 amazing chapters can be grouped into four fascinating themes:

1. **Materials and Substances:** Learning about all the different metals, minerals and elements used;
2. **Laboratory Design:** How to build the perfect ancient chemistry lab;
3. **Tools and Equipment:** The cool gadgets and machines they invented; and
4. **Measurements and Special Terms:** The specific language and scales used in experiments.

It's like a complete chemistry course, written by ancient Indian scientists!

Tiny Particles and Big Ideas

Before we dive in, let's look at the two revolutionary concepts that show how advanced these scientists were. Modern science has confirmed these ideas only recently:

- **The Science of the Super Small**: Modern medicine uses *nanotechnology* in many ways, including making sure drugs are sent to a targeted organ in the body. Without knowing the word *nanotechnology*, these ancient chemists created particles so small that they are measured in nanometres (billionths of a metre). If Earth were shrunk to the size of a marble, a metre would scale down to about a nanometre. Their special grinding, heating and mixing methods made nanoparticles (typically 15–50 nanometres) that were safer and more effective in the human body than larger particles – exactly what modern medicine strives to achieve today.
- **Making Metals Body-Safe:** The ancient concept of creating 'biocompatible' materials – substances that the human body can safely use – was groundbreaking.

Raw metals like mercury, gold, or copper can be dangerous if swallowed. But these chemists found ways to carefully purify and transform these materials into safe, healing forms called bhasma (ashes). The ancient chemistry wizards managed to remove impurities and change the particle size. They combined metals with other substances (such as herbs or minerals) to make new compounds – centuries before modern labs even existed.

O-O-O-O-O-O-O-O-O-O-O-O-O-O-O

Safety First

The ancient chemists were also careful scientists who had their own precautions and safeguards.

- *Heating and Quenching*: Materials were heated to high temperatures and rapidly cooled in special liquids (such as herbal liquids, oils or buttermilk, or other natural substances);
- *Grinding and Mixing*: Raw materials were ground with plant extracts or minerals to change their properties;
- *Purification*: Each material needed its own specific cleaning method or shodhana process;
- *Testing for Purity*: Several methods were used to verify that the materials could be used safely.

O-O-O-O-O-O-O-O-O-O-O-O-O-O-O

Chapters 1–4: Mercury, the Superhero Metal

The first four chapters are all about mercury, called pArada in Sanskrit. To these scientists, mercury was the star among metals, able to cure diseases and even help people live longer and healthier lives.

Now, you might be thinking, 'Wait! Isn't mercury dangerous?'

And you'd be right!

They too knew that mercury can be harmful, and they worked out ways to make mercury safe and useful.

- Chapter 1 introduces mercury and explains its special powers, such as the ability to transform other metals (that's what they believed).
- Chapter 2 explains how to test its purity and source.
- Chapter 3 describes how to clean it, by using plant juices like those of garlic and betel leaf or by mixing mercury with sulphur and rock salt.
- Chapter 4 reveals two magical transformations:
  - MAraNa (Calcination): Turning mercury into a fine medicinal powder through heating.
  - Bandhana (Binding): Safely combining mercury with other substances to make compounds like rasa-sindUra or vermilion (red mercury sulphide).

They even built special devices like the damaru yantra, shaped like an hourglass, to heat and cool materials precisely.

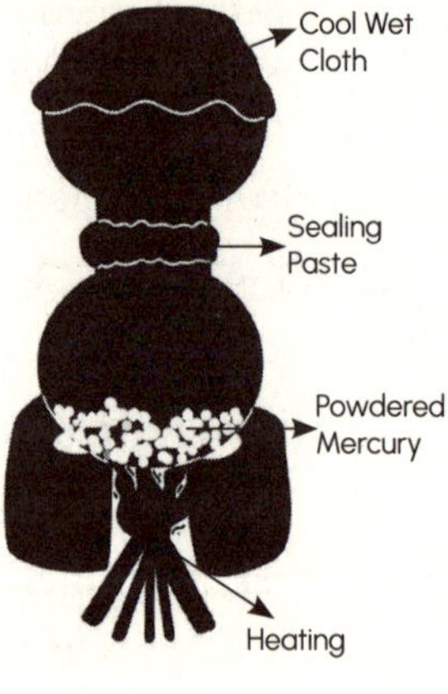

DAMARU YANTRA

Chapters 5–7: Mastering Other Metals and Lab Design

- Chapters 5–6: After mercury, they moved on to gold, silver, copper, iron and tin, each needing its own purification process.
- Chapter 7: This has the ancient laboratory blueprint – it describes

the rasashAlA ('chemistry house'), a carefully designed chemistry laboratory. It was squeaky clean, like modern sterile laboratories. Only trusted and trained people could work there, and had to follow strict rules and ethical guidelines.

It's a wonder how close this was to modern lab safety and 'Good Manufacturing Practices' (now known as 'GMP').

Copper Coin Shining Experiment

Make an old copper coin shine, using chemistry!

What You Need

* A dull copper coin
* Vinegar or lemon juice
* A pinch of salt
* Water
* A bowl or cup
* A soft cloth or tissue

What to Do

1. Place the copper coin in the bowl.
2. Pour in enough vinegar or lemon juice to cover the coin.
3. Add a pinch of salt.
4. Gently rub the coin or leave it in the solution for about one minute.
5. Rinse the coin with water.
6. Rub the coin dry with a cloth or tissue.

Wow! The coin looks brighter and shinier.

What's Happening!

The acid and salt remove the dull coating on the copper, and drying the coin helps the shine appear clearly.

Why It's Special

Ancient chemists used plant juices (like garlic or betel-leaf juice) mixed with minerals to purify metals. We used vinegar/ lemon (an acid) and salt.

Both methods use chemical reactions to remove impurities and restore the metal's shine!

Chapters 8–9: The Treasure Chest of Materials

The chemists divided their materials into three groups:

1. **MahArasa** or the primary powerhouses: These are eight important minerals, including mica, cinnabar, mercury and *shilajit* (a mineral-rich mountain substance).
2. **Uparasa** or the supporting cast: Secondary minerals that had their own healing properties.
3. **Ratna** or the precious gems: Diamond, pearl and other precious stones, believed to have healing powers.

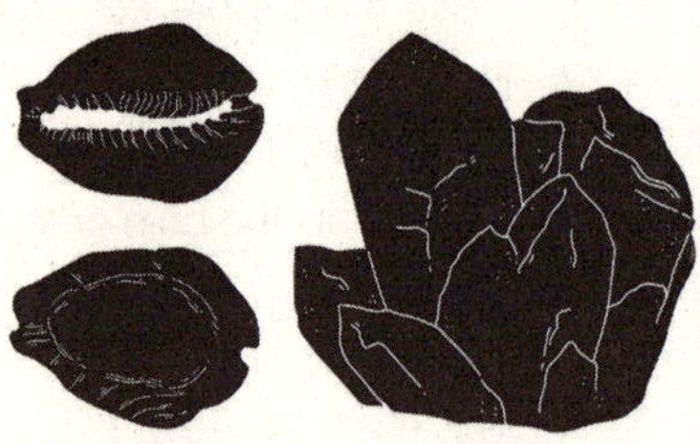

MINERALS AND COWRIE SHELLS WERE USED IN CHEMISTRY EXPERIMENTS

They also used sAdhArana rasa – 'helper minerals' like kampila for skin problems, gauripAshAna for breathing issues, navasAgara for digestion, kaparAdikA (from cowrie shells) for stomach and eye problems, and gIr-sindUra (red mercury compound) for chronic illnesses.

o-o-o

Chapters 10–11: Engineering Marvels

The final chapters describe the impressive machines and heating systems used. Their methods were precise, eco-friendly and surprisingly modern. They included:

- *Crucibles*: Seventeen types of heat-resistant clay pots, each designed for a specific purpose.
- *Yantras* (machines): These included the damaru yantra for sublimation (solid-to-gas-to-solid transformation), the koshThi yantra, which was a furnace reaching temperatures as high as 800°C and the vAlukA yantra, a sand-bath system for steady heat.
- *Revolutionary PuTa Heating System*: A temperature-controlled method using layered cow-dung cakes, with gajapuTa systems using 1,000 such cakes to generate temperatures of 800–1000°C.

Modern Science Confirms Ancient Wisdom

Scientists today have tested ancient bhasma with X-ray diffraction (XRD) and transmission electron microscopy (TEM). The results show that ancient chemists did create nanoparticles and safe compounds. Often using completely natural materials, their techniques formed early 'green chemistry'. In many cases, their techniques are more efficient and environment-friendly than many modern ones.

Be a Young Alchemist:
Create Your Own Safe 'Magic Powder'

Just like Acharya Rasa Vagbhata mixed minerals and metals 800 years ago, you can create safe 'magic powders' at home!

What You Need

- Turmeric powder (yellow)
- Baking soda
- A small bowl
- Lemon juice
- A spoon

What to Do

1. Mix one spoonful of turmeric with one spoonful of baking soda in your bowl.
2. Add a few drops of lemon juice.

Watch the magic! The yellow powder will fizz and turn reddish-orange.

What's Happening? Ancient chemists heated and mixed substances to change them. The lemon juice (acid) reacts with baking soda (base), creating bubbles, just like their experiments! The colour change shows a chemical reaction.

Why It's Special: Turmeric was used in ancient Indian medicine, and you've just done a real chemistry experiment like scientists did 800 years ago!

Safety Note: Always do this with an adult. DON'T taste any chemistry experiments.

The Magic Lives On

The *Rasaratna-samucchaya* proves that adventures in chemistry began many centuries ago in India! Today's scientists still study these ancient texts to find clues to making better medicines and working out how to deliver them efficiently in the body as well as safer manufacturing processes and technologies. The ancient Indian chemists proved that with curiosity, creativity and careful work, anyone can unlock the secrets of the universe, one chemical reaction at a time.

The magic of chemistry continues, and perhaps one day you'll be the next great chemist to discover something that helps make the world a better place!

The authors acknowledge the help of Dr. Malati Raghunath for this chapter.

4

ENCYCLOPAEDIA

MANASOLLASA

In your history class, you learn about kings, queens and their dynasties. You probably know about their battles, and the forts and palaces they built. But have you ever wondered what their lives were really like? What did they eat? What games did they play? How did they rule their kingdoms – all without phones, the internet or even newspapers?

Well, there's one magical Sanskrit book that tells us all this – and more! It's called *Manasollasa*, which means 'that which makes the mind happy'.

It was written by King Someshvara III of the Kalyani Chalukya dynasty around 1129 CE – almost 900 years ago! His kingdom included parts of present-day Karnataka, Andhra Pradesh, Telangana and Maharashtra.

A GIANT BOOK OF EVERYTHING

The *Manasollasa* has 100 chapters, divided into five big books (each called a vimshati or 'set of 20') that have 20 chapters each.

Book Name	What It's About	Chapters	Verses
RAjya PrApti KAraNa	Becoming a king and establishing a kingdom	20	308
RAjyasya Sthairya KAraNa	How to keep the kingdom strong	20	1,300
Bhartur Upabhoga KAraNa	The king's life at the palace	20	1,820
Pramoda KAraNa	Fun, art and celebrations	20	3,219
KriRA Vimshati	Sports, music and entertainment	20	1,375

Scholars say that only a handful of old copies of the *Manasollasa* survive today. The most complete manuscript is at the Baroda Central Library in Vadodara, Gujarat.

INSIDE THE BOOK

The book is a one-stop manual for rulers, an encyclopaedia of all that they should know.

Book 1: What Makes a Good King

The first book talks about what kind of person a king should be. A ruler needs special qualities to rule properly. Just like a doctor must know about medicine, a king must know how to take care of his people, like a caring father towards his children.

A good king must be brave and strong, but also kind and fair. He should listen to wise advisers who can help him make good decisions – those who are smart with money, others who are fearless warriors and yet others who know about healing and medicines.

The book warns that a king's life is always in danger, and that's why he needs loyal guards and his food checked for poison. There were officers with special jobs – one was called an 'asamphedya', someone who could never be bribed, and another was a 'kritamanyu parikshaka', a food taster who kept the king safe.

Book 2: How to Run a Kingdom

Ruling a kingdom is no joke! The second chapter talks about how a smart ruler should know how to manage his kingdom's money and resources, while saving something for hard times, just as a wise family saves for the future. The book mentions specific tax rates for crops, mostly about one-sixth of what farmers grew. Even honey and ghee were taxed! But the king was warned not to take too much, or the people would be unhappy.

The Mighty Elephants

Elephants were super important for kings in ancient India – they were the battle tanks of the time. They were strong and could frighten enemies. A king's power was measured by the number of elephants he had. The book explains different types of elephants – some were calm and gentle, while others could be trained for war, and taught to fight with their tusks and trunks. Even white elephants, considered very special and sacred, are mentioned.

Trainers used special words and commands to control elephants in the same way that we train dogs today, but the words were far more complex. Local command words from regions like Maharashtra and Gujarat are mentioned too.

Rivers

The book mentions many rivers, including the Ganga, Yamuna, Narmada, Tapi and Gautami. Rivers were important because people lived near them, and they used the water for drinking and farming. The king needed to know about the geography of his land to rule it well.

Jewels and Treasures

The text lists five special types of jewels that every king should own: diamonds, rubies, pearls, emeralds and sapphires. These weren't just for looking pretty; they showed how wealthy and powerful the kingdom was. The book explains where different types of pearls come from and how to tell good ones from poor ones. It lays down rules too – for instance, the king should not wear pearls that are too heavy.

A Strong Army for a Strong Kingdom

A king needed a strong army to protect his people from enemies. The *Manasollasa* explains how the army should be organized –

soldiers on elephants and horses, and foot soldiers armed with bows and swords.

The king should never trust his enemies and should always keep his army well-trained, even during peaceful times.

Learning from the Past

The book mentions that this information comes from older, even more ancient books. The author studied these old texts and combined their wisdom into this guide for kings. The text specifically says that meanings of certain words may be found in other books, like the *Vasantaraja Shakuna.*

Medicine and Health

Both chapters mention the importance of keeping people and animals healthy. It was the king's duty to make sure that there were good doctors in his kingdom who knew about different medicines made from plants. (Interestingly, all the medicines came from plants, not metals! See chapter 'Rasaratna-samucchaya' in the book.)

There were special doctors for people, and experts for animals like elephants and horses. The book even discusses how to treat fever in elephants!

Book 3: Royal Entertainment and Palace Life

The 'Bhartur UpabhOga KAraNa' section of the *Manasollasa* teaches kings about entertainment, art and how to enjoy life in the palace. It shows that being a king isn't just about serious work; however, there were guidelines for everything!

Building Beautiful Palaces

The chapter starts by talking about how to build proper palaces for the king and his family. Just as there are different rooms for different activities in our homes, kings needed special buildings for various purposes. Buildings called dhruva were meant to last forever. Palaces needed good air, lighting and a special room called chAtsuka for ventilation. The text includes detailed instructions about how rooms should be built – their proper measurements and the directions they should face – showing that ancient architects were very scientific about building design.

Before building any palace, the king must perform a special ceremony called 'vAstu pUja' to honour the land and its spirits. The building area was divided into 81 squares, and the king performed rituals in each one. Ancient people believed the land itself was sacred and had to be treated with respect.

The book says that the palace should be lit up with bejewelled lamps and beautiful decorations made of ivory, gold, crystal and precious stones. The walls should either be made of crystal slabs that look like mirrors or decorated with wonderful pictures. The text even mentions different types of beds – including a water bed!

The Art of Painting and Colours

The chapter teaches kings about painting and the various colours used in royal art. There are only four original colours mentioned: white, red, yellow and black. All the other colours were made by mixing these basic ones. White came from a conch-shell powder called shankha, reds were a combination of two ingredients called dArada-laktaka and gairika, yellow was made from something called haritAla and black from kajjala or lamp soot. Artists made golden decorations, using real gold called mishravarna.

Drawing the Human Body Correctly

One of the most interesting sections of this chapter teaches artists the skill to draw people properly by measuring body parts with a ruler. This is like using a special ruler to sketch a person, using a system called 'iconometry' – measuring with specific units.

The basic measuring unit is called an 'angula' (finger-width). Using this measure, artists can calculate all the other measurements. The text provides very detailed lengths and widths for 27 different parts of the body, from the crown of the head right down to the toes. This system helps artists make the people in their drawings look realistic and proportional. The measurements cover everything: where the eyebrows should be, how far apart the eyes should be placed, where the nose and mouth belong, and even the length of the arms and legs compared to the rest of the body.

Royal Entertainment and Festivities

The chapter describes many different types of entertainment that kings should enjoy. There are special seasons for wearing different clothes – silk in spring, white cotton in summer and various coloured clothes in different types of weather. The king should change his outfits according to the seasons, just as we all do.

The text describes elaborate bathing ceremonies where the king uses special perfumes and oils. Different seasons require different bathing rituals – in spring, the king should use fragrant oils like keshava, and in summer, he needs cooling treatments. There are special preparations made from things like camphor and sandalwood for different times of the year.

Royal Dining and Food

The text includes rules about how kings should eat and what foods are appropriate for different times. Kings should sip water often during meals to help with digestion, but they should never drink too much at once. There are specific foods suggested for morning, noon and evening, as well as for different seasons. The text gives recipes for special drinks and mentions that kings should understand the science of nutrition.

This third book shows that royal life in ancient India was highly organized and sophisticated. Every activity, from building palaces to eating meals, had specific rules and methods. The king was expected to be not just a ruler but also a patron of the arts, a student of the sciences and a person who understood the finer aspects of civilized life. This knowledge helped kings become better leaders because they understood beauty, culture and the proper way to live, which made their subjects respect and admire them.

Books 4 and 5: Games, Arts and Royal Celebrations

Both 'Pramoda KAraNa' and 'KriRa Vimshati' focus on entertainment, games and various forms of royal enjoyment. These chapters show that ancient kings needed to understand not just serious matters of ruling but also how to have fun and appreciate the finer things in life.

Royal Sports and Games

Kings needed physical exercise and sports, just like everyone else. The chapter describes various games and sports suitable for royalty, involving elephants and horses. One interesting game mentioned is similar to modern-day polo, played on a field that measured 400 by 400 units, with fencing all around. The game required eight players on each side.

Different Types of Entertainment

The chapters describe various forms of entertainment suitable for different occasions and seasons. Some kinds of entertainment were suitable for public occasions when the king needed to impress visitors and display his status. Other activities were meant for relaxation with family and close friends. The text emphasizes that a wise king knows how and when each type of entertainment is appropriate.

Wrestling and Physical Training

Wrestling was considered very important for royal fitness. The text describes different types of wrestlers and how they should be trained. Just like modern athletes, ancient wrestlers had to follow strict training routines for years and special diets to stay in top physical condition.

The king was advised to hold wrestling matches as entertainment; he also needed to keep himself physically strong to command the respect of his soldiers. Wrestling training helped develop courage, strength and quick thinking – all essential qualities for a good ruler.

Royal Vehicles and Transportation

Kings could use nine different types of royal vehicles for travel and ceremonies. Some were designed for comfort during long journeys, while others were built for impressive ceremonial processions.

One interesting vehicle mentioned is called 'dolapAka', which was like a palanquin or covered chair carried by men, while the 'pushpaka' was decorated with flowers and used for special celebrations. The text also describes vehicles for travelling on water and various types of boats for river journeys.

The choice of vehicle was important because it reflected the king's status and the importance of the occasion. A king arriving for a peace treaty might use a different vehicle from the one used for going to battle or attending a religious ceremony.

Music and Performance Arts

Music played a very important role in royal life. The text mentions that kings should understand the various types of musical instruments and appreciate good music. There were five special instruments that could create beautiful sounds when played together: bheri – a kind of drum; shankha – conch shell; kAhala – a wind instrument; mridanga – double-sided drum; and kAmsya-tAla – metal cymbals. The king should have skilled musicians who could perform during meals and other royal activities.

The various types of performances and shows suitable for royal entertainment included dance performances, storytelling and dramatic presentations that could both entertain and educate the audience about important stories and moral lessons.

Court Ceremonies and Protocols

The text provides detailed instructions about how court ceremonies should be conducted. When the king held formal audiences, there were specific rules about where different officials should sit, how they should dress and how they should behave in the royal presence.

High-ranking ministers and advisers sat closer to the king, while lower officials had designated places further away. The arrangement of the court showed everyone's rank and importance in the kingdom's hierarchy. Even the colours and styles of clothing worn to court were regulated according to each person's position.

During important festivals and ceremonies, the king should wear special ceremonial clothes and jewellery. The text describes how the royal umbrella should be held and how the king should be accompanied by his officials during public appearances.

Seasonal Activities and Festivals

Royal activities were organized indoors during the rainy season, while good weather allowed for outdoor sports and ceremonies. Spring was considered the best time for certain festivals and celebrations. The king was advised to participate in seasonal festivals that helped connect the royal family with the common people and the natural cycles of farming and harvest.

Education and Cultural Patronage

Kings were expected to be patrons of arts and culture by supporting musicians, artists, wrestlers and other skilled performers. This patronage helped preserve important cultural traditions and encouraged excellence in various fields. A king who could appreciate good music, skilled wrestling or beautiful art would be better able to judge quality and make wise decisions about supporting cultural activities.

Training Royal Children

The text includes information about how royal children should be educated. Princes and princesses needed to master serious subjects like statecraft and military strategy as well as learn to appreciate and participate in cultural activities. Young royals should excel at horsemanship, understand music, appreciate art, and play appropriate games and sports. This well-rounded education helped prepare them to become effective rulers who could connect with different types of people in their future kingdoms.

Managing Entertainment Expenses

The chapters also touch on the practical aspects of organizing royal entertainment. Kings needed to understand how much different types of entertainment cost and how to budget for various activities without squandering the kingdom's resources. A wise king learned to balance impressive entertainment that enhanced royal prestige with responsible spending that didn't burden his people with excessive taxes.

These fourth and fifth sections demonstrate that effective kingship required understanding all aspects of civilized life. A king who only knew about warfare and taxation but couldn't appreciate art, music or proper entertainment would not earn the full respect and loyalty of his people. The *Manasollasa* teaches that true authority comes from being accomplished in all aspects of leadership.

Royal Riddles

In 'KriRa Vimshati', the king is expected to hold games and tournaments periodically, involving riddles and puzzles to keep his mind sharp and creative. Here are some examples in the book. Can you solve them without looking at the answer?

1. 'What is the source and sustenance of all life?'
2. 'It fears not, it drives away, it has one eye and it shines by its own brilliance.' What is it?
3. 'When not in use, it sleeps in a sheath. It's called a piercer. When released, it goes fast but never returns.' What is it?
4. 'Always on the highway, without breath. It doesn't move, although used at the doorstep.' What is it?

o Answers: 1. Food (Anna); 2. The sun (Surya); 3. An arrow; 4. stone slab (on the doorstep or a milestone on the road)

Can you create some more like these? The more complicated round was of five questions that had the same answer! Can you try that? Here's one we created with three questions to give you an idea:

Question 1: I can take you to magic places, teach you about the stars, or help you sleep. Yet I never travel unless someone carries me.

Question 2: I have a beginning, a middle and an end. You may wander anywhere inside me and still know where you are.

Question 3: I can be fat or skinny, ancient or brand-new.

Answer: A book!

5

FARMING AND AGRICULTURE

KRISHI PARASHARA

Today, almost half the population of India works as farmers. They grow the food that everyone eats! In ancient India, people respected farmers greatly. Perhaps that was why this book was written. 'Krishi' means farming, and Parashara was a wise man from ancient India. This book tells us what Parashara knew about farming. What's interesting is that it is written as a poem! The book has 243 verses, all in Sanskrit.

Thank You, Food-giver

Not so long ago, children were taught to say, 'AnnadAtA sukhI bhava' after every meal, which means, 'May the people who gave me this food be happy.' This blessing includes the farmers who grow the food, the shopkeepers who sell it and the cooks who prepare it.

It's strange that India doesn't have more ancient books about farming. Many books like the Vedas and *Arthashastra* talk a lot about it, but only one Sanskrit book, *Krishi Parashara*, is known to be entirely about farming. People found three copies of this book in libraries in Tamil Nadu and West Bengal. They examined all three carefully and then published them with an English translation.

WHO WROTE THIS BOOK?

The book says Parashara wrote it, but that's probably not true. There's no author's name or date in the book. By studying the way it's written and the kind of language it uses, experts think it may be about 900 years old. Some parts mention someone called Raghunandana. Was he the writer? Or did he merely add a few lines? Or did he just copy or translate an even older book to make sure that it wouldn't be lost over time? Nobody really knows.

WHERE WAS IT WRITTEN?

This is a mystery too. People who have studied it think it might be from Bengal (now West Bengal) because the book talks about farming that needs a lot of rain – just like in the northern part of West Bengal. Some words in the book sound like Bengali. The book also talks about using oxen to help with farming, which is common in that region. But that's just a guess.

Although we don't know who wrote the book or where it came from, the writer was a skilled poet. The Sanskrit words fit together so well that they sound musical, even if you don't understand what they mean. Let's see what this special old book has to say!

INSIDE THE BOOK

The poet first prays to Prajapati – the god of creation – who later came to be known as Brahma. He says that even the rich must bow to the farmer for their food. Farming, he adds, is just as important as the king.

The Importance of Growing Crops

According to Parashara, rice – a staple food – sustains not only humans but also gods and rAkshasas. You may wear the most expensive jewellery, but without rice you would starve. That is why people must give due respect to rice, the farmer and agriculture.

Farming is sacred, and those who share the food that agriculture provides are like superheroes! So, the author says: share your food and don't waste it.

Will There Be Rain This Year?

Rainfall is very important for farming. We need to become rain experts to cultivate a good harvest. What does Parashara have to say about that?

Long ago, the calendar system in India followed the Saka Era, a historical Hindu calendar era, whose year zero corresponds to 78 CE. Each year, a different planet reigned as the 'lord'. This changed the rules for taxes and sharing crops.

The *Krishi Parashara* predicted the pattern of rainfall for each month according to the reigning planet. This helped farmers plan their work better.

Calculations are provided to forecast rainfall on a monthly basis. When the sun or the planets move close to certain constellations, rainfall is predicted. For example:

> In the month of Pausa (mid-December to mid-January), strong winds fromthe north or west indicate rain. However, if the wind blows from the east or the south, it means a drought is imminent. In the month of Chaitra (mid-March to mid-April), if the first new moon falls on a Sunday, the year will have normal to medium rain; if it happens to be a Monday, the rain will be torrential; and if it is a Tuesday, the year won't have enough rain.

Weather Detectives of Ancient India

Want to know if it's going to rain?

Ancient Indian farmers were expert weather predictors! When they noticed ants scurrying out of their homes, carrying their eggs, or peacocks dancing, or animals like cats and snakes running around in a frenzy, or heard frogs croaking loudly, these were sure signs that it was going to rain very soon. The ancients observed these peculiar animal behaviours and used them to accurately predict rain.

These farmers also looked at the stars and planets to predict rainfall for each month.

Our ancestors even used the direction from which the wind blew to tell if there would be rain or drought. No weather apps needed – just sharp eyes and clever observation!

If the farmer's portion = 1 unit (of the crop),
then the king's portion = 3 × 1 + 2 = 5 units;
and the minister's portion = ¼th of the king's share = 5 ÷ 4 = 1.25 units.

Thus, the farmer had to give away 6.25 out of every 10 units.

That sounds rather unfair to the farmer! One hopes that the king and the minister obeyed the teachings of books like the *Arthashastra*, which were specifically written for the ruling classes and warned them not to exploit the farmer.

Ee-i-ee-i-o: Animals in the Farm

In the olden days, animals did all the hard work in the fields – ploughing and tilling. In India, cows and bulls – called vAha in the text – did most of the labour. The author lists rules for caring for their animals – this includes good feeding, shelter and medicines. Any harvest reaped after ill-treating these animals would only bring bad luck.

He recommends the use of eight bulls to a plough. He clearly mentions the ideal size of the byre or cowshed and how important it is to keep it clean.

In the month of Kartika (mid-October to mid-November), he recommends a pUja ritual for the cows that includes smearing the cattle with saffron and sandalwood paste. He even mentions the most auspicious days and times to introduce new cows into the byre. He lists the uses of dung within the house and in the fields.

The Plough

This was the farmer's main tool. Made of iron and wood, it was used to till the soil and sow the seeds. The ancient book describes the ideal size and measurements of its various parts.

When the day and time are auspicious for ploughing, the text instructs the farmer to:

- Bathe, wear clean, white clothes and pray to Earth, to the planets and to the special gods, Prithu and Prajapati.
- Give gifts to the priest who helps with the ceremony.
- Anoint the tip of the plough with honey – so that the day is sweet!
- Finally, perform hala-prasAraNa – the first tilling of the soil.

Then the farmer selects a matching set of bulls for ploughing – a black set, a red set, or a red-and-black set – and applies butter on the sides of their faces (literally buttering them up for the hard work ahead!). The farmer then makes offerings and prays to Lord Indra for plentiful rainfall. Finally, the farmer lights a ghee lamp to Vayu, the wind god who brings the clouds. This is their way of asking for good luck with their farming.

All about Seeds

Magha (mid-January to mid-February) and Phalguna (mid-February to mid-March) are the best times of the year to collect seeds for sowing in the next season. The book has advice on how to dry the seeds and sort them by size. It also recommends storing them away from cattle, ghee, oil, buttermilk, lamps, salt or cooked food (can you guess why?).

The author suggests the best time to sow seeds – and when not to. Before sowing, the farmer must bathe, sow three handfuls of moistened seeds and pray to Indra. After the entire field has been sown, the farmer must look towards the east, pray to Mother Earth and offer her some ghee and pAyasam (sweet rice pudding).

Rules for root fertilizers and transplanting are also mentioned. Even the distances between plants for the crop when transplanted depend on the position of the stars in the lunar calendar. Kattana, or thinning the crop and removing the weak paddy, must be done only on certain days. Instructions are also given for when to weed and when to water.

Before water is stored in autumn, the farmer plants a reed called 'nala' in the north-east corner of the field on a Kartika Sankranti day and worships it with curd-rice and payasam. He then chants the prescribed mantras; there are also some special mantras in the book to keep pests away from the crop.

The Harvest Party Rulebook

After harvesting crops, ancient Indian farmers hosted amazing feasts! However, there were strict rules for the farmer to follow:

- Serve the oldest guests first.
- Serve pAyasam on banana leaves.
- Include tasty food items like curries, fish, meat and vegetable dishes. Include foods made with asafoetida and pepper.
- Also serve yogurt, milk, ghee and other dairy products.
- Remember to provide drinks, fruits and root vegetables.
- Make sure to serve lots of sweets.

The *Krishi Parashara* – in beautiful Sanskrit poetry – gave farmers detailed instructions to celebrate their hard work!

Harvest Time

The month of Agrahayana (mid-November to mid-December) is the right time to harvest crops. The author suggests to farmers that, on an auspicious day, they must wear clean clothes, be pure of mind and harvest a small part in the north-east corner of the field first. They should take the harvest home silently and place it in the eastern part of the home.

After harvesting has been completed, the farmer builds an elevated rectangular mud platform with a raised boundary ridge around it, called a 'medhi'. On a lucky day and time, a pole is erected in the centre. The oxen, tethered to this pole, trudge in circles around it to dehusk the rice. To measure rice, a vessel called ADhaka is used – it must be made of the wood of specified trees. The book also provides rules on when to store the rice in the granary.

The text ends with a request to Lakshmi, the goddess of wealth, to fill all the granaries with grain.

It reminds us that Parashara wrote this book on agriculture.

A LATER DEPICTION OF AN INDIAN FARMER WITH HIS PLOUGH

6

GOVERNANCE

ARTHASHASTRA

Is it easy to teach people who rule? Not really! But in ancient times, there was a man so knowledgeable that he wrote an entire book advising rulers how to run their kingdom efficiently and competently. The book was called *Arthashastra*. Artha means wealth – it could be money, a comfortable lifestyle or an activity that earns money. Since this book is meant for kings – how to get a kingdom and look after it – the focus is on wealth in the form of territory, economic activity or getting money for the king's treasury. The *Arthashastra* talks about the dos and don'ts for a king to be a successful ruler.

HOW WAS IT (RE)DISCOVERED?

One day in 1909, Rudrapatna Shamasastry (1868–1944), the librarian of Mysore's Oriental Research Institute, was going through some palm-leaf manuscripts. The manuscripts had been donated to the institute by a pandit from Thanjavur.

It was Shamasastry's lucky day.

Among the books, he found a text that had been considered lost. It was the *Arthashastra*. When he copied it out onto paper, he noticed some errors. The palm leaves were not in the right orde, and some of the verses needed explanations. He sorted these out and published the Sanskrit version in 1909 and then the English version in 1915. Since then, many have translated and published their versions of this rare book.

WHO WROTE IT AND WHEN?

The text identifies the author as Kautilya. A group of historians say that this author, Kautilya (his lineage name), was the same as Chanakya ('Chanaka's son'), the adviser to Chandragupta of the Maurya dynasty, and Vishnu Gupta (Chanakya's personal name). This debate continues.

In this book too, you'll find the authors rarely reveal anything more than their name. Perhaps they want us to focus on what they say and use it in our lives rather than learn about them.

There's a lot of confusion about the date too! Many dates have been given in the text – most of which are between the second century BCE and the first century CE. However, there are also some internal clues:

- It mentions silk from China. The word 'China' comes from the Qin dynasty, which began around 221 BCE. The text must be from well after this date.

- The text mentions trade in coral from the Mediterranean, which became popular only from the first century CE.
- The text mentions written documents – Sanskrit writing appeared around the first century CE as well.

We may never know the 'right' answer, but what we do know is that many parts of the *Arthashastra* are very helpful for us even today.

THE BOOK

As in most other books of this era, the *Arthashastra* is composed of two-line sutras. The words are extremely precise and often difficult to translate or even understand. Authors have relied on commentaries that explain them. One helpful commentary was found written in Malayalam. Isn't it amazing that this shAstra, just as many others in this book, was found across India in different forms? How difficult it would have been for people to travel in those days and make the effort to carefully preserve palm-leaf manuscripts for curious knowledge-seekers!

INSIDE THE BOOK

The *Arthashastra* has 15 books (parts) in total, divided into chapters.

In Book 1, Kautilya (who calls himself Vishnu Gupta here) says that this text is the essence of earlier books on the same topic. He lists the 15 books and their broad contents. Then he comes to the chapters within Book 1. Here's what they have to say:

Book/Parts	What It's About	Chapters
1. Training	How to train the king, ministers and officials	21
2. Activities of Superintendents	Managing taxes, resources and departments	36
3. Justice	Law, courts, punishments and fairness	20
4. Eradication of Thorns	Removing dangers to the kingdom	13
5. Secrets	Spies and secret agents	6
6. The 'Circle'	Neighbouring states and alliances	2
7. Six-fold Strategy	Planning peace and war	18
8. Calamities	Handling disasters and emergencies	5
9. Battle preparation	How a king gets ready for war	7
10. War	Battlefield tactics	6
11. Confederacies	Dealing with alliances and groups of states	1
12. The Weaker King	How a weaker king should act against stronger foes	5
13. Capturing a fort	Strategies to take or defend a fort	5
14. Top secret Practices	Hush-hush practices in ruling a kingdom	4
15. Writing a Treatise (like the *Arthashastra*!)	How to write and structure a work	1

First, it teaches that being a king is all about earning money, saving it, making it grow with wise investments and distributing it. In order to achieve this, agriculture, cattle-rearing and trade are vital. It's like your parents teaching you to think carefully before spending your pocket money!

The book says young princes should spend time with wise elders – learning from them, just as we do from teachers and other grown-ups. Interestingly, it warns princes that their biggest problems come not from enemies but from bad habits and choices they make. Self-awareness and self-control are their key mantras!

The book says kings need assistants (ministers and counsellors) to run kingdoms – like school principals needing teachers and other staff to run the school. Kings had to choose carefully, ensuring honesty and competence. Kautilya notes cleverly: 'Just as a vehicle can't run with just one wheel, a king can't rule a kingdom alone.'

A Quality Test for the King's Counsellors

Would Kautilya make you a counsellor in his kingdom? Here's his checklist. Rate each quality:

✓ if you have it 100%

Background and Influence

- ☐ Born or brought up with responsibilities
- ☐ Have natural influence over others
- ☐ Command respect in social situations

Skills and Training

- ☐ Proficient in multiple fine arts (e.g., music, dance and painting, among others)

- ☐ Strong communication and storytelling abilities
- ☐ Skilled in practical matters and daily tasks
- ☐ Well-trained in leadership fundamentals

Mental Attributes

- ☐ Display wisdom in decision-making
- ☐ Possess strong foresight and planning abilities
- ☐ Demonstrate quick intelligence and sharp memory
- ☐ Make firm decisions without wavering
- ☐ Show enthusiasm to take on responsibilities
- ☐ Act promptly without putting off things

Character Traits

- ☐ Maintain pure character and strong ethics
- ☐ Display dignity in all situations
- ☐ Show loyalty to principles and people
- ☐ Demonstrate excellent conduct with no complaints
- ☐ Possess qualities that attract rather than repel others
- ☐ Easy to work with and get along with
- ☐ Show genuine affection and care for others

Physical and Emotional Strengths

- ☐ Maintain strong physical health
- ☐ Display high endurance in challenging situations
- ☐ Show courage in facing difficulties
- ☐ Handle stress and pressure well

Relationship Management

- ☐ Build positive relationships with others
- ☐ Avoid creating enemies or antagonizing others
- ☐ Resolve conflicts diplomatically
- ☐ Maintain good relationships across all levels

Answer key:

All ✓s – you're a minister.

Between 10 and 27 ✓s – you're a middle-level counsellor.

9 and below – you're a lower-level counsellor.

There's a fascinating section about royal spies too! These were secret agents who helped keep the king safe and informed about what was happening in the kingdom. We are told where to recruit them, how one can test if the ministers and counsellors are loyal to the king, and how to reward the spies.

The book even has rules about how to have good meetings (like your class discussions!) and how to talk to people from other kingdoms. It was really important to keep the king safe from bad people who might try to hurt him, especially by poisoning his food. So they had special rules about protecting the king's meals (kind of like having a very strict food-safety inspector)!

How do you measure up to Kautilya's idea of a prince? Take this test!

The prince's timetable

- Mornings are for training to fight with weapons, as well as learning to fight while riding elephants, horses and chariots. Then the young prince has time set aside (like school periods) to listen to the Ramayana and the Mahabharata, and learn them. During this time, he would also study history, stories, fables with morals, law books and the *Arthashastra*.

  No new lessons after this – the evening time is dedicated to revising the morning's lessons and clearing any doubts he may have.

When is the student a good one?

– Has he listened attentively (sutra) to gain knowledge?

- Has he practised (yOga) that knowledge?
- From the practice, is he able to control his thoughts, words and actions (vidyA sAmarthyam)?

The prince's enemies are of two types:

The First Group of Challenges: feelings and thoughts

- Getting too angry (like when your little sister borrows your iPad without asking)
- Wanting too many things (like begging for everything you see in a store)
- Showing off too much (like bragging about getting the highest score in a game)
- Acting like you're better than everyone else
- Getting too comfortable and lazy (like when you think you're so good at maths that you stop practising)

The Second Group of Challenges: when your five senses trip you up

- Taste: Only wanting to eat your favourite fast food (and refusing to eat healthy stuff)
- Eyes: Getting stuck to screens all day
- Ears: Only wanting to hear people say nice things about you (and getting upset when someone gives you helpful advice)
- Touch: Always choosing the soft, easy, comfy stuff (like refusing to help with chores because they're 'too hard')
- Nose: Only wanting nice smells around you (and avoiding getting sweaty while playing sports)

Here's the cool part: the book doesn't say these things are bad! It's totally okay to enjoy video games, yummy food and comfortable things. The problem comes when that's ALL you want to do.

Think of it like this: if you only ever play video games, when will you learn to ride a bike? If you only eat sweets, how will your body grow strong? If you only want people to say nice things, how will you learn from your mistakes?

A true leader (or an awesome reader like you!) needs to find a balance. Enjoy the fun stuff, but also be ready to work hard, try new things and sometimes do things that aren't so comfortable. That's how you grow into someone really amazing! Kautilya gives examples of kings like Duryodhana and Ravana, who were really smart but were defeated by inner enemies. Can you say which ones?

What do you think? Is there anything from these two groups of challenges that you sometimes struggle with?

Book 2 deals with the jobs of government superintendents, who report to counsellors and ministers.

Some interesting remarks:

- The kingdom made money from farming, cattle-breeding, trade and forests. Everything needed protection by the army.
- Elephants were the ultimate war machines. Kautilya cared so deeply about them that he declared that a person found guilty of killing an elephant faced the death penalty!
- An ideal village, according to Kautilya, should have 100–500 families, with natural boundaries and plenty of water.
- The king had a special job: helping orphans, frail people and others who needed support.

Defences were super important! The kingdom's borders and capital needed strong forts. We're talking water forts, mud forts, desert forts and hill forts – each with moats and trenches, turrets and even roads for chariots.

He had specific rules about everything. Artisans making wool and cotton threads, bamboo mats, skins, armours, weapons and gauntlets had to live in the west. Every 10 houses must share one water well.

There were about 17 posts for ministers, and Kautilya explained exactly what they needed to know.

Kautilya loved measuring things precisely! Take the 'prastha' – an ancient Indian unit of volume, approximately equal to 768 millilitres (roughly 768 grams). One man's meal included 700–750 grams of rice, 180–200 grams of sUpa (pulses/lentils) and 45–50 grams of ghee/oil. Dogs were given 1 prastha of cooked rice per meal!

Taxes were calculated in mAsha – an ancient weight unit traditionally equal to 0.97 grams. A load carried by a cow or a horse cost 2 mAshas, while a big cartload was 7 mAshas.

Coins were important, and Kautilya devoted pages to explaining how to mine metal, create coins and test for fakes.

In some respects, Kautilya was surprisingly progressive for that era. For instance, he wrote that women who couldn't leave home could earn money by weaving. The agriculture chapter was mind-blowingly detailed – he even explained how to choose seeds based on water availability and cloud types. His calendar formula is still used in the Indian calendar today. The animal-care chapters are amazing! He gives detailed advice on caring for cows, elephants and horses. His tip for horses? Bathe them and dust sandalwood powder on them every day!

The chapters on spies are the most exciting! Anybody could be a spy. He recommended having spies disguised as thieves at every crossroads outside the towns, reporting on who was travelling where and why!

Book 3 focuses on law. Making agreements was serious business. Penalties for dishonesty were harsh – you couldn't pass off poor-quality land as good land. Only spies were allowed to make false statements! Kautilya recommended trusting evidence, cross-examination and sworn declarations.

Women's rights were a mixed bag for that time – they could own property, remarry if their husband died and leave a husband who mistreated them. In property sharing, the eldest sons got the best deal, followed by the younger sons; daughters only got what was left.

Punishments were severe! Not sharing water, damaging fields or blocking roads could get you into serious trouble. Slavery existed, but cheating slaves of their earnings was a punishable offence. (Yes, slaves could earn, save their money and even use it to buy their freedom, according to the *Arthashastra*.)

Interesting fines included those for:

- Calling people with disabilities hurtful names;
- Felling or damaging trees in public areas; and
- Throwing garbage into someone else's home.

Monetary amounts were in rUpa – the predecessor of today's rupee!

Book 4 explains how different groups could work together in harmony. But cause a nuisance…and you might get fined or even thrashed.

Natural calamities were a big deal. For food shortages caused by rats and locusts, Kautilya recommended domesticating cats and mongooses. He provided detailed post-mortem procedures for sudden deaths – creepy enough to inspire a detective story!

Government officials (including judges) faced serious consequences for shirking work or being corrupt – with penalties ranging from fines to dismissal. Jailers who locked up people without a fair trial weren't spared. As for thieves secretly tunnelling into a fort to steal and plunder…they were headed for a beheading!

Book 5 is all about the royal court. The king used spies to trick disloyal ministers, who might even poison the king! Taxes and salaries were carefully calculated. The heir to the throne got 48,000 paNam annually, while messengers earned merely 10 paNam (one paNam is thought to be approximately ₹5 today, but there are different views, considering we don't know exactly when this book was written).

Book 6 focused on sovereignty – a kingdom's freedom to decide on its actions. The king had to constantly control ministers, the country, the fort, the treasury and the army. These five parts were key to a kingdom's sovereignty. While much of this has already been covered in earlier books, Kautilya provides many suggestions on these topics in two chapters of this book.

Book 7 deals with survival, defence and the foreign policy of a kingdom, and outlines six ways to retain power:

1. Keeping peace;
2. Waging war;
3. Remaining neutral during conflicts;
4. Marching to threaten (not fight);
5. Making alliances; and
6. Strategic peace or fighting during others' conflicts.

Book 8 offers disaster-management advice. All calamities can be managed by the king and his ministers if the king is capable and healthy.

'Don't be greedy or act in anger,' Kautilya warns.

Book 9 focuses on defending the kingdom, suggesting that the king should be an expert in geography and climate. For example: 'Out of consideration for the people of the enemy country, it's imperative that invasions be made during their dry season and not their monsoon.'

His famous 3-step rule to resolve conflicts would be:

1. Try to come to a peaceful resolution;
2. Create competition; and
3. Use of force would be the last resort if the first two methods fail.

Book 10 covers war strategies – from camp construction to river-crossing techniques, such as using elephants, planks on pillars, bridges, boats and rafts made from dry gourds and baskets.

He even advises the king on what to say to motivate armies, and what doctors need for the medical care of the sick and the wounded. Battle positions are discussed in detail.

Book 11 is all about how to win over 'countries' of that time. In a way, the advice is about building alliances. Kuru and Panchala, which figure in the Mahabharata, are examples of how competing powers can becomes allies.

Book 12 tells the king how to deal with powerful enemies. The role of a messenger/ambassador is written down in detail. 'Build alliances for a strong fort,' exhorts Kautilya. He suggests using spies to regain power and isn't opposed to tricks such as a block of stone or wood above a doorway that falls on the enemies' heads (do NOT try this!).

Book 13 explains how to capture a fort, including ways to use spies. It even describes a recipe for an inflammable powder made from metals like zinc, specific flowers and hair!

Book 14 is about carrying out stealth attacks on the enemy. Some of these include vile-smelling smoke generated by burning a mixture of certain insects, fish and grains. Most of them are truly bizarre and creepy, like witches' potions. Some could blind the enemy; and others could eliminate hunger and thirst to help one's armies fight longer on the battlefield.

In **Book 15**, Kautilya summarizes why he wrote the *Arthashastra* and how it's organized. He explains the logic behind each chapter. Kautilya concludes that the *Arthashastra*'s purpose is to conquer wealth in this world and the next. He reveals his real name – Vishnu Gupta – and explains that he wrote this text to save the Nanda king from misrule and wrong advice from earlier books on this topic.

7

MATHEMATICS

LILAVATI

Did you know that 'LIla' means play, and 'Lilavati' is also a girl's name! Lilavati was a mind-blowing book on mathematics written by Bhaskaracharya and served as the standard textbook across India until the British rule. Talk about staying power!

This book isn't just smart – it's sheer genius. Each mathematics problem is actually a poem in Sanskrit with rhyming words at the end of each line. So Bhaskaracharya wasn't just a math wiz – he was also a poet in his own right and a brilliant teacher who made learning fun. All his poems are addressed to a girl; so – at a time when across the world, including on the Indian subcontinent, it was not at all common for girls to be educated – he felt that it was important that girls learn mathematics!

Mathematics connects to everything we do, and the 277 poetic problems in the *Lilavati* give us a fascinating glimpse into what life was like in 12th-century India. Bhaskaracharya was born in 1114 CE in Maharashtra and died in 1185 CE in Ujjain, Madhya Pradesh. Besides being a math genius, he was also a top-notch astronomer – and most probably the head of the astronomical observatory in Ujjain!

The Legend of Lilavati

The great mathematician Bhaskaracharya predicted that his daughter, Lilavati, could only marry at one precise auspicious moment.

He built a special water clock – a vessel with a tiny hole at the bottom and a floating cup designed to sink exactly at the right time.

But, as a curious Lilavati leaned over to watch, a pearl from her necklace accidentally fell into the vessel, blocking its hole. The cup never sank. The perfect moment passed, and the wedding couldn't happen.

Heartbroken, Bhaskaracharya consoled his daughter by naming his famous mathematics book after her.

Through hundreds of beautiful math problems, Lilavati's name became immortal – remembered by students for over 800 years.

Did this really happen? Many people believe it did... What do you think?

Can you try and make a water clock?

THE BOOK

Lilavati isn't just any book – it's part of a collection of four incredible works by Bhaskaracharya, collectively called

'Siddhanta Shiromani' (which means 'Crown of Books'). The collection includes:

- *Lilavati* (on arithmetic and geometry);
- *Bijaganita* (on algebra); and
- *Graha Ganita* and *Gola Adhyaya* (both on astronomy).

The 277 sholkas of the *Lilavati* are arranged into 34 step-by-step chapters, starting from basic arithmetic and going on to advanced mathematical concepts.

The *Lilavati* teaches mathematics through clear explanations, clever puzzles and real-life problems. It makes learning numbers, fractions and geometry feel like solving riddles rather than studying a textbook.

The other texts of the 'Siddhanta Shiromani' are equally fascinating and detailed, and the topics mentioned below are only a part of the remarkable storehouse of information recorded in it.

Ingenious Inventions and Discoveries

First there are Bhaskaracharya's mind-boggling math inventions and contributions:

The Chakravala Method: Bhaskaracharya created a brilliant and clever step-by-step math trick to solve very hard number puzzles like $3x^2 + 5x + 7 = y^2$. These puzzles were so difficult that mathematicians in Europe didn't figure out methods like Bhaskaracharya's until about 500 years later. It's like he had a mathematics superpower far ahead of his time!

Early Calculus Pioneer: Calculus is a branch of mathematics that helps us understand change, like how fast something is moving or how a curved line bends. About 500 years before polymaths Isaac Newton (in England) and Gottfried Leibniz (in Germany), Bhaskaracharya was already using ideas like these:

- **MadhyamAharaNa** – He created a method that helps find what is happening at one exact moment, like how fast something is moving right now, not just over a long time. The word 'madhyama' means 'middle', and 'haraNa' means to remove, because the method removes the middle term of a problem to make it easier to solve special equations with 3 terms. By removing the middle term, you reduce the 3 to 2.
- **An early version of Rolle's Theorem** – Bhaskaracharya discovered smart ways to find special points on curved lines, such as where a curve changes direction (this is advanced stuff even in today's mathematics classes).
- **Concepts of derivatives:** Bhaskaracharya used these to measure tiny changes in time and motion, helping to track small movements. These ideas later became part of calculus. Basically, he developed calculus concepts long before calculus was a thing!

Understanding of Zero, Negative Numbers and Infinity

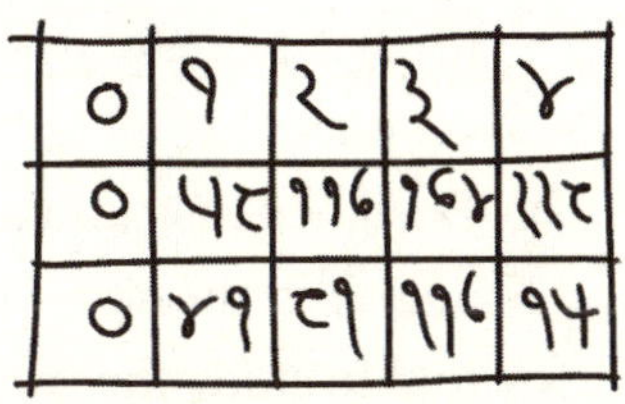

- Bhaskaracharya was among the first mathematicians to use zero and negative numbers correctly (when many people couldn't even imagine what negative numbers meant!).
- He recognized that dividing by zero gives infinity, describing it as 'a quantity which remains

unchanged no matter how many times it is divided or multiplied' (mind = blown!).

A Genius with Equations

- The Kuttaka Method solves tricky number puzzles like $5x + 7 = 3y$, turning impossible-looking problems into solvable ones.
- Solutions to Pell's Equation ($x^2 - Dy^2 = 1$), which had puzzled mathematicians for hundreds of years. *Fun fact*: it's called *Pell's Equation* by mistake – Pell didn't actually invent it.

Breakthroughs in Geometry

- Formulas for calculating the area of cyclic quadrilaterals (four-sided shapes that fit inside a circle), useful in advanced geometry!
- Trigonometric identity – a special mathematics rule connecting angles and triangles. It explains how different ways of measuring angles (called *sine* and *cosine*) are related, making tricky angle problems easier to solve.

Achievements in Astronomy

- Calculated the length of Earth's year as 365.2588 days (modern value: 365.256363), off by just about 3–4 minutes per year! How's that for precision!
- Created the Graha Spashta technique to accurately predict planetary positions (basically a GPS for planets, centuries before GPS was invented!).
- Designed instruments like the phalaka yantra to measure angles in the sky – kind of like a homemade astronomy tool to study the sun, the moon and the stars!

- Built a detailed model of the planets and calculated their movements with amazing accuracy – almost like mapping the solar system using only his brain and mathematics.

Trigonometry Mastery

- Created precise sine tables (see page 17 of the chapter on *Aryabhatiya*) that made navigation and astronomy calculations much more accurate (helping ships navigate and astronomers map the stars).
- Developed advanced trigonometric methods still important today (some of the same ideas students learn in school now!).

Mathematical Education

- Wrote *Lilavati* and *Bijaganita*, famous mathematics books that explained complex ideas through stories and puzzles (making mathematics fun nearly 900 years ago!).
- One of the first mathematicians to make learning maths engaging and enjoyable! (He would've been the coolest mathematics teacher ever!)

Bhaskaracharya accomplished all this in the 12th century, proving that brilliant mathematical thinking was happening on the Indian subcontinent long before many of these concepts were 'discovered' in the rest of the world. His work combined practical problem-solving with deep theoretical insights in a way that still inspires mathematicians today.

While there are colleges and research institutes named after him, Bhaskaracharya's contributions are mostly unknown to mathematics students in schools. Let's now dip into a few poems from the *Lilavati* and look at how he explained complicated problems through stories and puzzles. These poems aren't just clever – they make mathematics come alive.

INSIDE THE BOOK

Bhaskaracharya first prays to Lord Ganesha and says his book will be loved by smart people because it is clear, short and makes for interesting reading (and singing too!).

Here's the low-down on some of the many important topics he covers:

Basic Arithmetic

1. **Definitions and Tables**: This chapter contains many poems about the units of measurement, including coins, length and weight. Many of these words were used until just a few decades ago. Here's an example of how time was measured:
   - nimesha: the time it takes to blink once.
   - tatpara: 1/30th of a nimesha.
   - truTi: 1/100th of a tatpara.

   There are further units! In another system of measurement:
   - 1 Asu (a complete breath) is the time taken to recite 20 long vowels
   - 6 Asus = 1 pala
   - 60 palas = 1 ghatikA
   - 60 ghatikAs = 1 ahorAtra or divas (day)

- 30 days = 1 mAs (month)
- 12 months = 1 varsha (year).

2. **Place Values of Digits**: Bhaskaracharya used positions of digits from right to left as units, tens, hundreds and so on. We all use this today. Europe actually learnt this from the Arabs, who had learnt it from India. In this chapter, he gives names for larger numbers, such as abja for a billion. These made it easier to calculate larger values faster.
3. **Addition and Subtraction**: Bhaskaracharya teaches us the right method to write down the numbers in their proper decimal places and then add or subtract. Here is his verse:

aye bAle, LIlAvati, matimati buddhi-sahite,
dvipancha-dvAtrimshat tri-navati-shatam tadashta-dasha
shatopetam etAnyuta-viyutaschApi vada me
yadi vyakte yukti-vyavakalan-mArge'si kushalA || XIV ||

(O, you smart girl, Lilavati! If you're skilful in addition and subtraction, tell me the result when the sum of 2, 5, 32, 93, 100, 8 and 10 is subtracted from 10,000.)
The right answer for addition is 250. For subtraction, it is 9,750.

In mathematics, you learn about positive integers and negative integers. This concept was first invented in India, but it didn't reach Europe until the 16th century. That idea came from Indian mathematicians like Bhaskaracharya.

4. **Methods of Multiplication and Division**: Here, he teaches four different ways to multiply and one way to

divide. One method breaks numbers into parts, multiplies each part and then adds the results together.

5. **Eight Rules about Zero**: The important ones are:
   - if 0 is added to a number, the result is the same number;
   - when you multiply a number by 0, the product is 0; and
   - a non-zero number with zero as the divsor is called khahara, and is related to the concept of infinity.

⊕•⊕•⊕

Advanced Number Operations

Squares: Bhaskaracharya taught three ways to find squares, which help in finding the area of a room or calculating the costs of items in large quantities. One method splits a number into two parts and combines them smartly to get the square after adding twice the product of the two parts. For example:

297 = 290+7

$(290)^2$ = 84,100 and $(7)^2$ = 49

2 x 290 x 7 = 4,060

84,100+49+4,060 = 88,209

- **Square Root**: Square roots help find lengths and distances. They find practical use in various fields, like geometry (calculating distances and lengths using Pythagoras's theorem), physics (in equations of motion and distance formulas) and computer science (in algorithms and data transformations).

  Bhaskaracharya explained clear steps to find them.

- **The Cube**: He also taught three ways to find cubes, useful for finding the volume of solid objects (and even wind

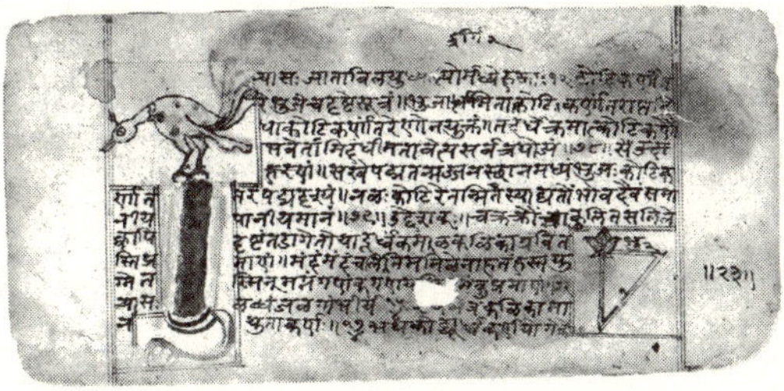

A PAGE FROM THE *LILAVATI* (FROM 1650), SHOWING THE USE OF PYTHAGORAS'S THEOREM IN THE CORNER

speeds). Cube roots, which are important for builders and architects, were also explained.

⊕•⊕•⊕

Fractions

Fractions are important in daily life – for telling time, using money and cooking. They're also the basis for more complicated mathematics. The verses deal with five different topics in fractions:

- **Eight Operations on Fractions**: Bhaskaracharya explained eight ways to work with fractions. These include simple fractions and mixed fractions, where a whole number and a fraction are together, like 7½. He showed step-by-step rules for adding, subtracting, multiplying and dividing these kinds of fractions in the correct order.
- **Addition and Subtraction of Fractions**: By using a common denominator and cancelling common factors, just as we do today!
- **Multiplying Fractions:** multiply the numerators together and the denominators together; then place the product of the numerators over the product of the denominators.

- **Dividing Fractions:** By using the 'reciprocal' (turning the fraction upside down): he says that division of one fraction by another is equal to multiplying the first by the reciprocal of the second.
- Squares, cubes, square roots and cube roots of fractions are also explained.
- This is one of the sums he asks us to solve. (If you do, your intelligence is as sharp as a blade of kusha grass, he says!)

  $5 \div 2^1/_3$

  [The answer is 15/7]

⊕•⊕•⊕

Algebra and Equations

Algebra helps find unknown numbers (unknown variables) and is useful in science and travel calculations. The various topics Bhaskaracharya deals with are:

- **Reverse Process**: How to work backwards to find unknown values by reversing division, multiplication, addition and subtraction.
- **Unknown Quantity**: To find this, he says, assign an alphabet to it. We use *x*, but he used *ya* in Sanskrit. Then do the operations given in the problem – multiplication, division, addition and subtraction. Next, multiply the alphabet by the result and divide the product by the number obtained before and, hey presto, you'll get the unknown.
- **Method of Transition:** Here, he gives us the rules to find two numbers whose sum and difference are given. Add and then subtract the given numbers and divide them by 2 to get the two numbers.

For example, if the numbers are a and b, $s = a + b$ and $d = a - b$, then $a = \frac{s+d}{2}$ and $b = \frac{s+d}{2}$

This formula is given for square numbers also.

- **Quadratic Equations**: These problems help find distances and heights, such as how far or high something goes when it's thrown or launched. Here, the problems are very imaginative: One problem talks about how Arjuna, in a fit of rage, flings a fistful of arrows to kill Karna. One has to find out the exact number of arrows he snatched up. In another problem-verse on bees, one bee gets trapped in a lotus flower, and the other bee feels sad – and more such imaginative clues help us learn quadratic equations!

Proportions and Applications

Bhaskaracharya taught proportions, which are useful in buying and selling. This included the 'rule of three', where you know three numbers (or values) and find the fourth, like figuring out how the price changes when the weight changes. He explains this using everyday items bought and sold during his time, such as saffron, camphor and rice. Today, we call this 'direct proportion'.

He also teaches 'inverse proportion', where one thing goes up and the other goes down. For example, going faster means reaching your destination sooner. In other words, increase in travel speed = reduction in travel time.

While we usually solve problems with just three values (price, amount and item),

Bhaskaracharya showed us how to handle much more complex problems – some with several values. His examples also show how barter, trade and interest worked in those days.

⊕•⊕•⊕

Combinatorics and Progressions...whaaat?!

Combinatorics is the branch of mathematics focused on counting, arranging and selecting objects, as well as finding the number of ways to form collections or sequences (like permutations and combinations). Bhaskaracharya taught clever ways to arrange things in order.

Permutations help when *order* matters, like arranging books in a sequence; and combinations help when order doesn't matter – like selecting a team from a larger group.

He explains this with fun verses in rhyme about real-life problems, such as a king designing a palace with many doors and windows and figuring out the air-circulation movements when different doors and windows were open or closed.

One problem uses what we now call Pascal's triangle – a number pattern shaped like a pyramid where each number is the sum of the two numbers above it. Indian mathematicians knew of this long before Bhaskaracharya or anyone else in the world mentioned it.

Bhaskaracharya wrote several verses about geometry and measurement, which were very important for farming. He described methods to measure land, containers and heaps of grain. In order to measure heights and shadows, he used ideas from the *Shulba Sutra*s, which include the rule we now call the Pythagoras's theorem – which was known in India long before Pythagoras's time, and was used for building and navigation at sea.

Here's one example:

> In a lake there were a large number of geese and cranes. A lotus whose height above the water surface was one vitasti (½ hasta or hand span), and its tip, bent by a rustling wind, sank at a distance of 2 hastas.
>
> O mathematician! Tell me quickly the depth of water.

He also gives the formula to calculate the volume of a ditch filled with water. This would have been very useful for farmers in those days who watered their fields with the help of ditches and trenches, and needed to share the water.

Bhaskaracharya ends the *Lilavati* by saying that anyone who learns all these formulas and their applications would be happy and prosperous. This verse has a double meaning: Lilavati, who has learnt all this, will make some lucky man very happy and prosperous (when she eventually marries).

Another verse, which some say was added later, mentions that this was written by Bhaskaracharya, who was an expert and had written eight books on grammar, eight on medicine, eight on logic, five on mathematics, one on the four Vedas and other important sources of knowledge. At the end of the *Lilavati*, Bhaskaracharya humbly thanks God, and reminds us that learning is vast and humans are always students.

8

MEDICINE

SUSHRUTA SAMHITA

Can you believe that a person who lived more than 2,000 years ago described plastic surgery! Yes, believe it or not!

It's described in a text called the *Sushruta Samhita*. 'Sushruta' means 'one who has heard correctly', and 'samhita' is a collection of information – like a personal library. If you noted down a lot of things that you thought were important from websites, books and conversations, and compiled them all in a notebook, neatly ordered by topic, that would be your Samhita!

In ancient India (and we're talking about 2,300 years ago), medical practitioners were divided into five types:

- *Rogaharas*: doctors
- *Shalyaharas*: surgeons
- *Vishaharas*: poison removers (toxicologists)
- *KrityAharas*: those who worked on mental illness (psychiatrists/psychologists)
- *Bhishaga-Atharvans*: curing with the help of sacred hymns, rituals and offerings to restore bodily balance

Warning! Any medicine should be taken only if prescribed by a proper doctor. Make sure you don't try anything from medical books like these by yourself!

This book is mostly about surgery and surgeons. A surgery that is well done can cure a person and even save a life. To this day, surgery is a complicated part of medicine, and we must be proud that centuries ago we were already good at it.

WHO WROTE IT AND WHEN?

Sushruta remains a mystery to us. We don't know whether that was his real name or even whether the book was written by just one person or several others added to it over time. Based on some words in the text, experts think it might have been first created about 3,235 years ago! The book even mentions that some parts were much older and were being written down then because they were useful.

In those days, books were handwritten on palm leaves or tree bark, so many people made copies. Nagarjuna, a chemistry scholar who wrote the *Rasaratnakara*, made a version that most people use today. The oldest copy we have is now in archives in Kathmandu, Nepal, and dates to 878 CE (yes, it's more than 1,140 years old!).

WHY IS IT IMPORTANT?

Many people use the principles and methods of Ayurveda to stay healthy. This book is like an instruction manual for Ayurveda. Some of its highlights are:

- **Surgery from Long Ago**: Even today, when doctors operate on bodies, it can be tricky. It's amazing that more than 3,000 years ago, Indians could do surgeries with simple tools.
- **First Skin-fixer-upper**: The book talks about fixing skin by moving it from one part of the body to another part to cover wounds or burns (skin-grafting). No other medical practitioner of that ancient time (pre-600 BCE) thought of true skin grafting. Sushruta was the first to do grafting in the world! The later doctors learnt the basics from this ancient book, even though they used different methods.
- **Eye Doctor Pioneer**: Eyes are very delicate parts of the body, and Sushruta wrote detailed instructions about eye surgery. In fact, he was the first person ever to do this.
- **Learning about Bodies**: Sushruta even explained how to remove parts of arms or legs (amputation) when necessary. He thoroughly understood anatomy and how the body worked. He taught his students to practise dissecting bodies by training on vegetables, dead animals and old wood.
- **Helping Babies Be Born**: Delivering babies is complicated even today. Sometimes babies get into tricky positions inside a mom's womb. If a doctor makes a mistake, it can be really dangerous. Sushruta had lots of helpful advice about this too!

Shall we explore what's inside this impressive book?

INSIDE THE BOOK

The *Sushruta Samhita* is an ancient Sanskrit book that explains surgery, medicine, anatomy and healing in a detailed and practical way.

Parts/Name	What It's About	Chapters
1. SUtra SthAna	Basic rules of medicine, surgery, tools and medical training	46
2. NidAna SthAna	Causes, symptoms and early signs of diseases	16
3. SharIra SthAna	The human body, anatomy, growth and development	10
4. ChikitsA SthAna	Treatments, medicines and cures	40
5. Kalpa SthAna	Poisons, toxins and their antidotes	8
6. Uttara Tantra	Special medical fields such as eye care, ear-nose-throat, children's health, mental health, and emergencies	66

Part 1: SUtra SthAna

According to Sushruta, Ayurveda comes from divine origins. There are four types of illnesses:

- Those caused by things outside your body.
- Those caused by problems inside your body.
- Illnesses of the mind.
- Illnesses caused by an imbalance of 'dOshas' in the body. DOshas are three physiological forces within all of us – VAta/VAyu (like wind/air), Kapha (like bile produced in the liver) and Pitta (like mucus, or phlegm). Each of

us has these in different proportions, which is why, in Ayurveda, people get different types of medicine even if they suffer from the same illness.

The text tells us who can learn and practise Ayurveda, and when it should not be taught. What's wonderful is that people from all social groups of the time could learn it, although this wasn't so for all branches of learning.

The text says one should not learn Ayurveda early in the morning, in the evening, or on days of the full moon and new moon. Chapter 6 also talks about this.

Chapters 5, 7, 8 and 9 tell us about surgery.

Chapter 10 explains what special skills a surgeon needs. This is the most important part of the text. This is why Sushruta is so famous.

There are eight types of surgery:

1. Cutting (Chhedya)
2. Opening (Bhedya)
3. Scraping (Lekhya)
4. Puncturing (Vedhya)
5. Searching or probing (Eshya)
6. Taking things out (AhArya)
7. Draining fluids (VisrAvya)
8. Stitching (SIvya)

The text provides detailed instructions on how to prepare the operation theatre, what tools are needed and what to do and not to do. It also tells you what to do after the operation. Based on his descriptions, some of the surgical instruments would look like those on the facing page (these drawing are from a 1907 book, *An English Translation of the Sushruta Samhita in Three Volumes*, by Kaviraj Kunja Lal Bhishagratna).

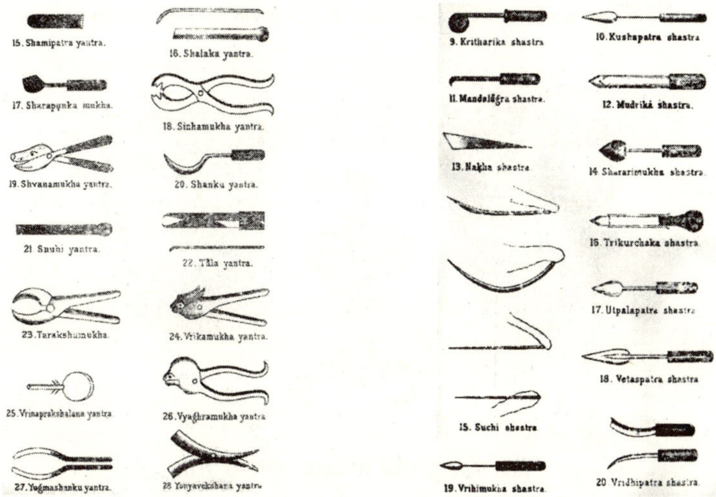

SURGICAL INSTRUMENTS BASED ON THOSE DESCRIBED BY SUSHRUTA

Chapters 11 to 20 are like a doctor's magic recipe book! They describe special potions for the skin before cutting it (ouch!), the way to seal wounds with heat (like a wizard!), bandaging injuries, and watching out for what lumps and bumps may tell us about what's happening inside the body.

In Chapters 21–32, we learn about three very important body energies called VAta, Kapha and Pitta. When these go out of balance – BOOM! – you might get sick. These chapters list clues to spot health problems and how to fix them with surgery. There's even a spooky part about what your dreams might mean. Imagine knowing what your nightmares are trying to tell you!

Chapter 33 talks about the trickiest illnesses that even the smartest doctors couldn't fix back then.

Chapter 34 has special instructions for taking care of kings when they're out with their armies because even

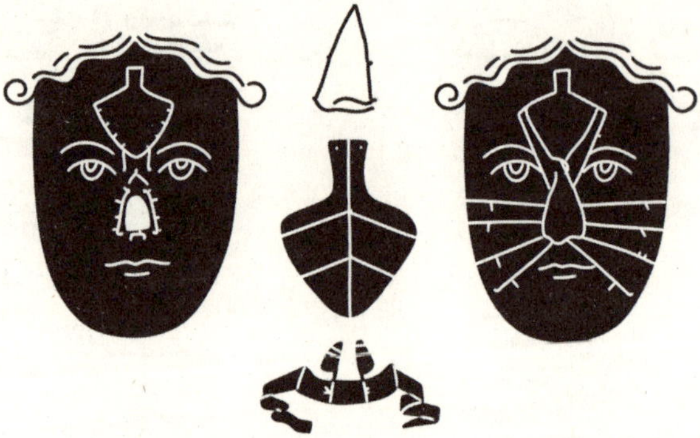

The Original Indian Nose Job

You've heard of people getting 'nose jobs', which they believe make them look better, but guess who invented it for those who had their noses chopped off during a battle or as a punishment? Yes, it was Sushruta!

He developed the earliest recorded method of rhinoplasty (or nose reconstruction), described in the *Sushruta Samhita*. How was it done?

- Skin was taken from the cheek (or forehead) while keeping a small, attached piece (or 'pedicle') for blood supply.
- The skin flap was stitched into place on the nasal stump.
- Two small tubes (often made from the castor-oil plant) were put into the nostrils so that the patient could breathe and the shape of the nose was maintained.
- The graft was treated with powders of liquorice, red sandalwood and barberry. Then, it was covered with cotton and bathed in sesame oil.

This laid the foundation for modern plastic surgery, and it was so effective that it was later adopted and improved in the 18th and 19th century as the 'Indian Method of Rhinoplasty'.

kings get sick! It also describes the qualities that make a good doctor.

Chapters 37–46 are the most exciting, full of curious medicinal concoctions. These ancient doctors were so clever that they knew little things, like bitter foods could make you very thirsty and hungry. And that plants growing in different soils would make different kinds of medicines. This ancient book is like having a time machine to see how doctors worked thousands of years ago.

Part 2: NidAna SthAna

In this section, the text discusses diseases of the nervous system, conditions like haemorrhoids, open wounds that take time to heal and diseases that affect the mouth, among others. While describing how to fix broken bones, the author splits them into two types:

- dislocations (where bones move out of place); and
- breakages (where bones actually crack or break).

The author even sorts these into more specific groups.

You can tell that the writer was very careful and thorough because there are detailed instructions about what to look for and how to treat each type of problem.

The book shows how people who had lived so long ago knew so much about the human body and had figured out different ways to treat all these problems, even without modern tools like X-rays or microscopes. They used their eyes, hands and the knowledge passed down from teacher to student to help people get better.

Part 3: SharIra SthAna

This section begins with an explanation about the deeper meaning of Ayurveda. According to the author, it's not just about treating illnesses and giving medicines, but the complete science of living a healthy life.

The author explains how our bodies are made up of the same five elements that exist all around us in Nature and how closely connected we are with our environment. We're made of the same stuff as the world around us!

When talking about how babies are born, the writer says that mothers need to be kept calm and happy when they're expecting a baby. This is because their worries and feelings can pass on to the baby growing inside them. Amazingly, the description of how a baby develops from the sixth month onwards is almost exactly the same as what modern science tells us today!

In addition to nerves, veins and muscles, the texts list special points in the body called 'marmas', or vital points. These marmas are taught at an advanced level in traditional Indian martial arts like Kalaripayattu (Kerala) and Silambam (Tamil Nadu). What makes these marmas special? If someone hits or presses these points with enough force, it can completely paralyse a person – sometimes forever! It's fascinating that Sushruta's knowledge is still being used today.

●•●•●

Part 4: ChikitsA SthAna

These chapters discuss the diseases discussed in Part 2 in more detail and variety, with unique complications doctors may see in particular cases. One chapter discusses hygiene:

Sushruta says we must all brush our teeth. He describes how to fashion twigs for use as toothbrushes and what the toothpaste should be (it includes honey!). He gives us recipes for mouthwashes and eyewashes. We are asked to oil and comb our hair regularly, and have oil massages. Recipes for the oils are provided too.

Sushruta constantly reminds us that food and treatment depend on the climate as well as the person's dOshas. 'Drink less water in the monsoon,' he advises, 'and more hot water in summer.'

●•●•●

Part 5: Kalpa SthAna

Sushruta lists the cures for various types of poisons from insect stings, snakebites and rats. Poisonous water and plants are also discussed. He issues a special precaution to the king: it is very rare to find a loyal person, so the king must watch out for poisoned food and drink.

Sushruta has good advice on kitchen design and the kitchen staff. The kitchen has to be large, airy and very clean, with many netted windows to keep birds (and we guess, flies) away. Flammable material must be carefully stacked and the god of fire, Agni, worshipped daily. Cooks and their helpers must be clean-shaven, with clipped nails and turbaned heads – and they need to smell good too! All of them are to be supervised by the kitchen doctor, who ensures that the king's food and drink aren't poisoned.

Feed a part to birds and see if they live. 'Burn a little,' he says. Poisoned food crackles loudly when set on fire and changes to the colour of a peacock's throat. It emits stinking fumes too.

Part 6: Uttara Tantra

Chapters 1–19 talk about all the diseases in different parts of our eyes (even our eyelashes!). Eyelids injuries? The author recommends surgery and then sewing up the cut with – guess what! – horsehair.

Chapters 20–24 are about diseases of the ear.

Then the book discusses head problems ranging from headaches to mental illnesses.

Next, there are several chapters about how the nine planets (or Nava Graha) can affect us.

Chapters 39–59 cover treatments for fever, jaundice, hiccups, excessive thirst and other ailments. The author also tells doctors to pay attention to how medicine tastes because it's important to make patients feel better. Different tastes can treat different kinds of ailments.

The last few chapters discuss mental illnesses and general rules to stay healthy, all based on what to eat and drink depending on the season.

Some advice:

- In cold weather, avoid dampness.
- Ride an elephant to avoid street water splashing on you.
- Don't eat unless you're hungry.
- In summer, enjoy water gardens and avoid spicy, sour and salty foods.

- Sleep in a bed of flowers.
- Drink some milk with sugar in the night before bedtime (it worked for them somehow, but what are your parents going to think about that?).

He ends with a glossary of important words, mentioning the chapter/s in which they're discussed.

Tomatoperate!

Sushruta described 'AhArya' – how a surgeon carefully removes things from the body without causing damage.

Your Challenge: To remove a tomato's seeds.

- Cut the tomato in half (ask an adult to do this).
- Using only a toothpick, remove as many seeds as possible.
- **Goal**: Do not break the tomato flesh!
- **Timer**: Give yourself 3 minutes.

Counting:

1. Seeds removed: ________
2. Times you broke the flesh: ________
3. Success rate: ______%

How to calculate your success rate:

No. of seeds removed

Divided by no. of seeds removed + no. of times you broke the flesh

x 100

How did you do? Surgeons often need to remove something (like a splinter or growth) without damaging the healthy tissue around it!

9

MEDICINE

CHARAKA SAMHITA

If you thought that health and fitness were a new fad, guess what! In ancient India, health experts followed a system called Ayurveda – which means 'the science of life' and is all about staying healthy and living your best life! It was divided into six parts:

1. **Internal medicine**: Treating what's wrong in your body.
2. **Surgery**: Operations to fix a problem.
3. **Head-and-neck medicine**: Treating everything from your collarbones up (like your head and face).
4. **Paediatrics and childbirth**: Caring for babies, children and everything related to birth.
5. **Toxicology and microbiology**: Handling poisons and those tiny germs that make you ill.
6. **Preventive medicine and nutrition**: Keeping your body VERY healthy even when you're not ill – plus studying the reason for why we REALLY crave more food sometimes (like when you just can't stop eating chips!).

Over time, doctors became experts in specific areas, but everything was eventually grouped into two main groups: medicine and surgery.

This awesome book is ALL about medicine.

THE BOOK

Would you believe we have medical knowledge from about 1400 BCE? That's about 3,400 years ago! Then came Charaka, who lived sometime between the fifth century BCE and second century CE (yep, sometime during those 700 years). He took all this brilliant information and organized it into a collection called the *Charaka Samhita* – which many consider the greatest book on medicine ever written.

The funny thing is, we know almost nothing about Charaka himself – probably because he cared more about keeping us healthy than talking about himself!

Charaka's Brain-Busting Quiz!

How much do YOU know about what Charaka taught? Let's find out with this quick quiz!

Question 1: True or False?

Charaka thought the body and the mind were wholly separate things.

A) True

B) False

Answer: *B. Charaka knew that the body and mind were deeply connected, and the mind plays a HUGE role in both falling ill AND getting better!*

Question 2: What special word did Charaka use for 'logical thinking' in medicine?
A) Shakti
B) Yukti
C) Mukti
D) Bhakti
Answer: *B. Charaka said doctors must use Yukti – logical thinking based on evidence, not just wild guesses!*

Question 3: According to Charaka, doctors should:
A) Never talk to other doctors
B) Be secretive about what they know
C) Meet and share ideas with other doctors to get smarter together
D) Work alone to avoid confusion
Answer: *C. Charaka believed doctors should exchange knowledge to improve their skills!*

Question 4: Charaka believed that all human bodies are:
A) Exactly the same
B) Like machines that work the same way
C) Different from each other, needing individual attention
D) Impossible to understand
Answer: *C. Charaka knew that every person is unique and needs customized treatments!*

Question 5: How many things did Charaka say doctors should check before giving medicine?

A) Just 1 thing

B) 5 things

C) 10 things

D) 100 things

Answer: *C. Doctors had to check 10 different factors about both the patient AND the medicine before writing a prescription.*

Question 6: What did Charaka think about the body's own healing power?

A) It doesn't exist

B) It's very important – don't give too much medicine!

C) It's not as good as medicine

D) Only works for colds

Answer: *B. Charaka believed the body has amazing healing powers – sometimes, it just needs a little support!*

THIS BOOK GOT *REALLY* POPULAR!

Charaka's ideas were so brilliant that his book became a huge hit among a lot of people! Later, scholars from various regions of India – like present-day Jammu and Kashmir, Gujarat, West Bengal, Maharashtra and Kerala – added on more chapters with their own local knowledge. Many others also wrote explanations to help people understand the tricky bits and shared their own cool experiences. These books are called commentaries.

INSIDE THE BOOK

The *Charaka Samhita* is HUGE! It has 9,295 verses written in Sanskrit. And when translated into English? It's over 300,000 words – that's like reading three to four Harry Potter books! This epic book is divided into eight sections with 120 chapters – that's a LOT of health wisdom!

Part	What It's About	Chapters (AdhyAya)
1. SUtra SthAna	Basic rules of health and medicine	30
2. NidAna SthAna	Causes and signs of diseases	8
3. VimAna SthAna	Testing and diagnosis	8
4. SharIra SthAna	The human body and its development	8
5. Indriya SthAna	The senses and warning signs of illness	12
6. ChikitsA SthAna	Treatments and healing methods	30
7. Kalpa SthAna	Medicines, herbs and preparations	12
8. Siddhi SthAna	Successful treatments and procedures	12

Part 1: Sutra Sthana: The Super-Cool Basics

Once upon a time, it is said, diseases started causing big trouble for great sages, making it difficult for them to study and live happily. The wisest ones – those who could control their minds like superheroes – meditated deeply and called upon Indra, a VERY powerful god.

Indra, being very knowledgeable, taught them Ayurveda – the ultimate knowledge about diseases, how they are caused, what they look like and how to zap them away! Many brilliant sages passed on this fantastic wisdom, and a genius named Agnivesha organized all this information in a logical way.

The first part of the *Charaka Samhita* starts with – what else! – the body!

Your Body's Three Power Types

According to Ayurveda, our bodies have three dOshas or special energy states:

- VAta – Quick and light like whooshing air and vast space. People with lots of VAta are slim, full of energy and bendy like gymnasts! But watch out – they can catch sniffles, get tummy troubles and feel restless easily.
- Kapha – Solid and steady like the mighty earth and flowing water. People with lots of Kapha are caring, patient as a tortoise and calm as a pond. They have strong bones, but they could gain weight faster than other people and sleep for long periods, like a hibernating bear.
- Pitta – Fiery, powerful and always ready to take on a challenge! Linked to flickering fire and rushing water, Pitta types are very focused, have great digestion and loads of energy. But they can be impatient, hangry and sometimes moody like a rainy day.

Magic Medicines and How They Work

Ayurvedic medicines follow the 'balance' rule – you need the opposite 'energy' to restore harmony. Too much fiery

Pitta? You need cooling Kapha medicines. It's like fighting fire with water!

The book describes loads of different medicines and where they come from. Most are made using plants found in our gardens and forests, but some use special minerals and animal products too. 'Evacuatives' are a special type of medicine that helps the body flush out bad stuff (yes, through poo and pee!). It might sound funny, but it's actually a brilliant way for the body to cure itself.

Ayurvedic medicines come in many different forms:

- Powders (mixed with water, ghee or honey);
- Pills (easy to swallow); and
- Sticky mixtures (gooey but powerful!).

Food: Your Body's Fuel

Ayurveda says that the food we eat can either make us feel energized or turn us into sluggish sloths – yikes! That's why we should:

- eat just the right amount – never stuff ourselves like a teddy bear at a tea party!
- go easy on heavy foods like flour-based treats, sugar-cane goodies, dairy and meat.
- think before we eat – consider how much we've been running around and how good our digestion engines are before we dive into our food.

Taking Care of the Body = Your Most Important Duty

Just like good citizens help their country (by recycling, by being kind and by following rules), we must do our duty to our bodies:

- Oil hair for a shiny, healthy glow.
- Get massages to keep muscles relaxed and happy.
- Bathe regularly to stay fresh and clean.
- Wear clean clothes to feel fresh and confident.
- Use a little perfume or jewellery – because feeling good matters too!

Seasonal Eating – The Summer Edition

Just as we dress differently for each season, we should eat differently too. For instance, during summer, the sun slurps up water from Nature like it has a giant straw, making everything hot and dry. That's why cool and sweet foods are perfect to keep our bodies happy.

- Drink lots of cool, sweet drinks (imagine you're a plant).
- Eat rice with milk (yummy and cooling).
- Don't eat too many salty, sour, spicy or hot foods (they make you even hotter).
- Avoid doing heavy exercise (save your marathon running for cooler weather).
- Take catnaps in a cool, shady spot during the day – just like a sleepy lion!
- Sleep somewhere breezy at night – let the cool air tickle your toes.
- Splash cool water and apply sandalwood paste on yourself for an instant refresh.

- Visit shady forests and flower gardens – they're not just pretty, they keep you cool too!

Team Health Power

Ayurveda talks about how important it is for doctors, patients, medicines and helpers – The Ultimate Superhero Team – to work together to defeat disease. Everyone has a role to play:

- **Doctors** – Should be kind to patients and only treat illnesses that can be cured. (No wasting time and money on diseases they know they can't cure.)
- **Patients** – Must follow the doctor's advice and take care of themselves. (Good health = Team effort).
- **Medicines** – These work like magical potions to fight off illnesses – but they need to be used wisely.
- **Helpers** – Nurses, assistants and even musicians and storytellers help keep patients in a happy, healing mood. (Imagine having a storyteller at your doctor's office – how much fun would THAT be?).

And there's more! This section ends with detailed notes on food, diseases and treatments that will make your head spin with wisdom!

Part 2: Nidana Sthana – Medical Mystery Solving

Get ready for eight action-packed chapters about disease 'detection' – how to spot diseases early – because the sooner we catch the symptoms, the better we can treat the illnesses! Besides fever (the body's red alert that bigger trouble may be brewing), some rather complicated conditions are covered, such as those to do with mental health, tuberculosis and epilepsy (when someone's brain sends their body mixed-up signals that can make them behave, move, feel or act in an unusual way for a short time).

Part 3: Vimana Sthana – Taste Adventures!

Get ready for eight jam-packed chapters that explore the flavours of life – literally! Did you know that what we eat can change how we feel? This section of the book tells you how different tastes – sweet, salty and bitter – affect the energies that make our bodies tick.

The Four Types of Foods

1. Eatable – Things you munch on
2. Chewable – Things you chomp on
3. Drinkable – All your favourite liquids
4. Lickable – Like ice lollies

The Perfect Meal Formula

Your plate should have three magical parts:

1. Food to eat
2. Drink to wash it down
3. The right balance for your dOsha type

There's more! This section also dives into epidemics (when a disease spreads super-fast across a large number of people in an area), disease that go from bad to worse and even 20 types of tiny troublemakers – pathogens! – that make us sick. And yes, doctors must check phlegm, poo and pee.

Never Stop Learning

Charaka reminds doctors to keep learning forever and to study the right knowledge. Science is all about observation and clever thinking, after all.

Part 4: Sharira Sthana – The Amazing Human Body

Charaka saw eight elements that make up the human body – the interesting thing is that even in those ancient times he included not only skin, blood, flesh (muscle), fat, bone and so on, but also the psyche (or mind).

He talks about what makes a human remarkable:

- **A Brilliant Mind** – helps you think, dream and imagine!
- **Ten Superpowered Sense Organs** – eyes like an eagle, ears like a bat, nose like a bloodhound, taster tongue, feeling skin, chatty voice, grabby hands, walking feet and so on.
- **Five Magical Sense Powers** – seeing cool stuff, hearing amazing sounds, smelling yummy (or yucky) smells, tasting delicious food and feeling everything around you…

- **Prakriti (the body's building blocks)** – Earth, water, fire, air, space, mind, intelligence and your sense of 'you'.

Charaka explained how all these bits work together. According to him, humans are actually made of the same stuff as the world around us – water (like in rivers), earth elements (that's what makes our bones strong) and fire (that's the warmth you feel in your tummy after a hot meal).

Our organs and senses connect the inside world to the outside world, just like bridges. When everything works right, we feel fantastic! But if a bridge breaks down – yes, we fall ill.

Control Your Senses: Stay Healthy

Charaka warns: too much of anything – such as sweets – can make us ill! Even Kautilya, the famous thinker behind the *Arthashastra*, agreed with this – great minds think alike!

This section then tells the story of how a baby grows! They had figured out – WITHOUT fancy microscopes – how a tiny embryo (smaller than a full stop!) grows into a baby. It even has special advice on what pregnant mums should eat based on seasons and body types.

Then it goes into incredible detail about each body part, starting with your skin, bones (a whopping 360 in all, including your teeth sockets and nails!) and loads more, such as the ligaments, muscles and all the squidgy bits. Ancient doctors got pretty close to what modern science knows today.

Part 5: Indriya Sthana – Body Detective Work

WARNING: Charaka says these 12 chapters are *only* for experts. He warns us to never go to a doctor who doesn't know their stuff. Yikes! The signs he talks about are based on skin colour, the sound of the voice and examination of various parts of the body. The list is MEGA long, but the main point is: we must always keep a sharp lookout for even tiny changes in the body and mind (which are connected like best friends). When we notice weird changes, we should check with the experts right away.

Part 6: Chikitsa Sthana – Treatments and Cures

This huge section has 30 chapters for loads of different illnesses, with all the medicines needed, how much to take and notes on how to mix the ingredients to make the medicines.

This section includes everything about building a strong body that fights off nasty germs. A popular medicine for this is chyawanprAsh – and this is where the secret recipe is hidden! Other problems that get fixed include feeling tired and bored, fevers, feeling too heavy, diabetes, skin problems, mental-health issues, epilepsy, chest wounds (probably for warriors after battle), swellings, tummy troubles, anaemia, hiccups, asthma, coughs, extreme thirst, poisoning and many more. This section is very important for those who want to become Ayurvedic doctors.

Part 7: Kalpa Sthana – Secret Potions And Lotions

These 12 chapters are like an extra-detailed version of the previous section. It tells you where to find all the special plants needed for the medicines and how to prepare them properly. It's like a recipe book for medicines.

Part 8: Siddhi Sthana – Becoming Super-Healthy

In these 12 chapters, Charaka says that the body needs to flush out yucky stuff before it can take in new medicine. This is still a key principle in Ayurveda today! But too much flushing can be harmful – even dangerous!

Also, this depends on your body type, the weather and your health issues. It's a bit like pressing the reset button on your tablet – if you do it wrong, you might lose all your important game progress! So, it's a tricky job that needs a lot of careful thought.

Unlike other ancient books, this one doesn't have a proper 'THE END', but experts think we probably have the whole text exactly as it was written.

10

MUSIC

SANGITA RATNAKARA

'SangIta' means music and 'ratna' means jewel. Yes, you guessed it! This book is a special treasure about Indian music!

When babies are born, they cry – that's how we first learn to communicate. Later, we make different noises (sometimes animal sounds!), and then learn words, letters, and how to read and write. Maybe you know more than one language (which is brilliant!) or perhaps you can sing too! Sounds and music are everywhere around us and can change how we feel – happy, sad or excited. This book tells us all about this.

WHO WROTE IT AND WHEN?

There's a town called Daulatabad in the northern part of Maharashtra with a really impressive fort. A long time ago, it was called Deva Giri, which means 'hill of the gods'. The Yadava kings reigned there.

One of these rulers was King Singhana, who ruled from 1210 to 1247 CE, around 800 years ago. In his royal palace worked a very clever man named Saranga Deva. He was brilliant at medicine, music and poetry, all at the same time! This smart man wrote the *Sangita Ratnakara.*

At the start of his book, Saranga Deva tells us that he came from Kashmir. His grandad, Bhaskara, moved to Deva Giri to escape invaders. His father, Sodhala, worked for the king, and later Saranga Deva did the same. The Yadava kings truly loved music and medicine, and Saranga Deva was excellent at both! He was also very good with numbers and helped keep track of the kingdom's money. In his book, he starts off by boasting about his skills (just to make sure we know he's the right person to teach us!), but by the end, he becomes quite modest.

This book was written about 800 years ago. and within 100 years, many people all over the Indian subcontinent had read it, thought it was brilliant and written their own notes about it. Even today, anyone who wants to learn about Indian classical music must read this book. Shall we explore what's in it?

INSIDE THE BOOK

There are seven chapters in the *Sangita Ratnakara.*

Chapters	What It's About
1 Svaragata AdhyAya	Basics of sound, notes, microtones and scales in music
2 RAga Viveka AdhyAya	Different rAgas (melodic frameworks), and how they are built and used
3 PrakIrNaka AdhyAya	Various practical music topics like singing styles and performance techniques

4	Prabandha AdhyAya	Musical prabandhas (compositions) and poetic metres
5	TAla AdhyAya	TAla (rhythmic cycles) and how rhythm works in music
6	VAdya AdhyAya	Musical instruments and how they are played
7	Nartana AdhyAya	Dance, including body movement and expressive gestures

Chapter 1: Svaragata AdhyAya

Did you know that Indian classical music is like a magical recipe with two super-important ingredients?

1. **Notes or Swaras**: These are like the colours that make up a beautiful melody called a rAga. A rAga is special because it can make you feel different emotions when you hear it – happy, sad, peaceful… (Psst! Read the chapter on the *Natya Shastra* to know more about how music creates these feelings in us.)
2. **Beat or TAla**: This is the rhythm or speed of the music. It's like the heartbeat in our bodies that keeps everything moving along.

When people sing, they mostly focus on the notes, while instruments like the veena, flute and sitar help create beautiful melodies. Drums, like the mridanga and tabla focus on keeping the beat. Both parts (melody and rhythm) are equally important and crucial to making proper music.

Everything Starts with Sound

Saranga taught that everything in music begins with sound, which is called 'nAda'. He had a special formula:

SangItam = GItam (vocal music) + VAdyam (music from instruments) + Nrittam (dance)

He divided music into two types:

- **MArga**: This follows strict rules from the ancient book written by Bharata, the *Natya Shastra*.
- **Desi**: This is more like local music, which doesn't strictly follow all those rigid rules but is still wonderful to listen to.

Saranga believed that sound is the beginning of everything. Amazingly, he said this centuries before scientists came up with the Big Bang theory, which suggests that the universe began with an explosive sound! He explained that sound connects us to everything around us, including Brahman – a universal magical energy that's in everything. He believed that sound is an echo of that universal energy.

Inside Our Bodies

Saranga knew a lot about how our bodies work. Do you wonder why? He considered the human voice as the first and most important instrument, so he made it his business to know about the human body. He described how babies grow inside their mummies, and knew exactly when the skin and brain form in the womb. He even knew that a mother's feelings affect her baby's health and personality. He counted 900 snAyus or fibrous tissues in the human body (modern anatomy does not have a fixed number for these). He said we have 500 muscles, although today's scientists think there are more than 600 of them. He also correctly said that most of our body is made up of water.

Energy Points and Music

Saranga Deva described 10 special energy points in our bodies called chakras. These chakras help us connect to ourselves, the world around us and the magical Brahman energy he believed was inside us. And guess what helps us make these connections? Sound and music, of course.

He explained that when we make sounds, the power comes from just below our belly button, travels to our heart, throat, brain and then emerges through our mouth. 'Na' means life and 'da' means fire, so 'nAda' (sound) is the fire of life that keeps us and the world alive!

The Science of Musical Notes

According to Saranga, there are 22 types of sounds called 'shrutis' (which means 'what is heard'). From these come seven special notes or 'swaras' that you will recognize: SA, Re, Ga, Ma, Pa, Dha, Ni.

These notes can be high, medium or low – just like when you shout or whisper! Some notes even sound like animal calls! When you put these notes together in special patterns, you create a rAga. Saranga lists and explains many of these rAgas.

Saranga was brilliant at both music and maths. He figured out all sorts of ways to organize these notes into beautiful patterns that musicians still use today.

Chapter 2: RAga Viveka AdhyAya

Here Saranga classifies 264 rAgas into various groups. If you're learning classical music, you might like to create a quiz from this, learning to identify every rAga. Saranga liked all kinds of music, so he included Desi ragas too.

Chapter 3: Prakiranaka Adhyaya

Saranga says that music might be good, but to make people really feel something, the song and its words (lyrics) are very important. He says the best composers or 'vaggeyAkAra' need to be brilliant with languages, know lots of words (have a large and rich vocabulary) and know what they mean, be clever enough to choose the right words, be debate champions, have a logical way of thinking, understand how people feel and act (empathize), write songs quickly when needed and have many other skills. Of course, they need to be excellent at music too.

Checklist for a Good Singer
(Based on Classical Indian Vocal Standards)

Tick those you think apply:

[ ] Good at singing different types of songs like ragas

[ ] Expert at singing prabandhas (songs that people have written)

[ ] Knows how to make up music on the spot but still follows the rules

[ ] Can naturally do voice shakes and decorations (gamakas) at all voice levels
[ ] Has excellent control over their voice
[ ] Understands musical timing (tAla)
[ ] Pays attention and doesn't get tired when singing and practising
[ ] Knows about notes, songs and other music-related stuff
[ ] Good with lyrics
[ ] Has a clear voice
[ ] Practises and exercises regularly
[ ] Is careful about how fast or slowly to sing
[ ] Has a good memory
[ ] Can control breathing while singing with feeling
[ ] Able to make the audience watch and listen
[ ] Gains the admiration of music experts
[ ] Has a nice voice that sounds good
[ ] Good at starting songs or performances

Saranga says other people have to say their singing is good (it's not enough if the singers think so themselves!). And these other people need to know music well too!

Did you read about the dOshas in the chapter on the *Charaka Samhita* in this book? Saranga uses the three dOshas to categorize different types of voices as well.

The next time you listen to an Indian classical music singer, observe how their voice shakes in a controlled way. This is called gamaka, and Saranga says this is the hallmark of a great singer. He explains why and how singers must do this. Lots of practice and knowing the theory (chapters 1 and 2) are just two of his suggestions. He sorts gamakas into more than 36 types!

Finally, he gives a checklist of what matters when many singers perform together in a concert. Here's his checklist as a quiz. Can you guess the answers without looking at them?

Vocal Ensemble Quiz

Let's see if you know what makes a great singers' group!
Circle True or False for each question.

1. When singing in a group, you should listen to and follow the lead singer. *True / False*
2. In a good vocal group, everyone sings in the exact same way. *True / False*
3. It's important for everyone to follow the same laya and tAla. *True / False*
4. When someone makes a mistake, the other singers should help cover it up. *True / False*
5. Good singers can only sing in one voice range. *True / False*
6. In the best groups, everyone's voices/instruments sound similar together. *True / False*
7. Singing in a group means you can sing however you want. *True / False*
8. A vocal group needs a conductor to sound good. *True / False*
9. It's okay to sing louder than everyone else in your group. *True / False*
10. Listening to each other is an important skill for singing groups. *True / False*

Answers

1. *True – Following the lead singer helps keep the group singing together.*

2. *True – This is about uniformity in style.*
3. *True – Keeping rhythm (tAla and laya) is essential.*
4. *True – Covering errors helps maintain the performance quality.*
5. *False – Good ensembles can operate in three registers.*
6. *True – Voice similarity helps create a blended sound.*
7. *False – Group singing requires coordination.*
8. *False – Many vocal ensembles follow a lead singer.*
9. *False – Balance is important.*
10. *True – Empathetic following requires listening.*

Chapter 4: Prabandha AdhyAya

So far, we have looked at music (gIta) based on the rules created by the ancients. Now, we will look at music from local and regional areas that doesn't always come from ancient sources but is still enjoyed by people. This second type is called gAna. It's based on the Desi style of music.

Prabandha means 'well-knit' – and in this context it means a song where the words and music are very closely connected. A prabandha or song must have three or four parts to it, and they must all be interconnected. Saranga Deva loved to organize everything! His different ways of ordering prabandha are quite tricky for us to understand. But if you're really interested in writing songs and music, they're very important in terms of the choices you have.

He ends again with a list of dos and don'ts for singers and composers.

Chapter 5: TAla Adhyaya: Rhythm and Beats

Did you know that in music and dance, rhythm is just as important as melody? In Sanskrit, we call this tAla! TAla means the beat or rhythmic cycle. Just like your heartbeat has a regular pattern – dhak-dhak dhak-dhak – music also has a pattern that repeats. The Sanskrit word tAla comes from 'ta' (sound) and 'la' (motion) – so it means moving with sound! Talas not only keep the music alive and people clapping but also ensure better coordination with the singer, the dancer and the instruments. It's like teamwork with sound!

Saranga Deva lists many types. The most important ones are:

- EkatAlam – 1 beat (like clapping once)
- rUpakam – 3 beats
- Jhampa – 10 beats
- tripuTa – 7 beats
- Adi TAla – 8 beats (very popular in Bharatanatyam)

Each tAla is like a dance-step pattern. You have to maintain the beat while you dance or sing! This is done using claps, waves or counting on one's fingers.

Chapter 6 – VAdhya AdhyAya

Saranga Deva talks about two main instruments: the veena and the flute.

A veena is like a singing string, an instrument that you play by plucking its strings. It has a big, round body and a long neck. The vamsha or flute is like a whispering breeze! The veena produces sound when its strings vibrate. The flute makes sound when air vibrates inside it. Just like ripples in water, sound travels in waves!

Perfect Pitch – Size and Sound

Did you know that the size of the flute changes the sound?

A longer flute has a deeper sound.

A shorter flute produces a higher sound.

Try this!

Cut two straws – one long, one short. Blow into each like a flute. Which one has a higher note?

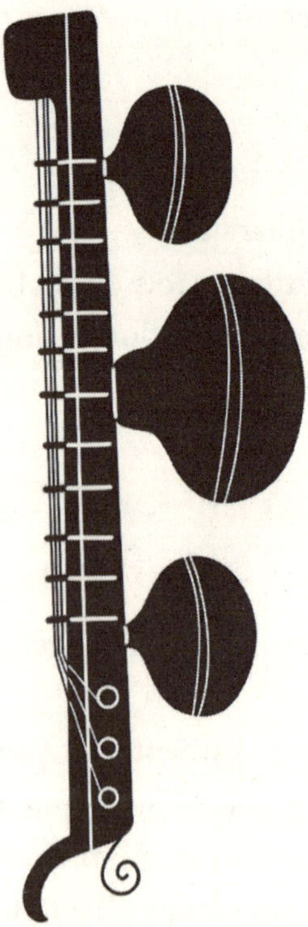

Good flutes have clear, sweet sounds. Bad flutes may have cracks, wrong hole sizes or dull sounds. Another instrument he mentions is the kinnari veena. It's a fancy kind of veena that's decorated and sounds heavenly. Some say it was played by celestial musicians called kinnaras!

Saranga says that instruments have to resonate – which means they should let sound flow and stay for a while, like an echo in a cave! Clap once and listen. Do you hear the sound stay for a second?

That's resonance!

THE HORSE-HEADED HEAVENLY MUSICIAN TUMBURU LEADS AMONG THE CELESTIAL MUSICIANS OR GANDHARVAS IN HINDU MYTHOLOGY, AND IS SHOWN HOLDING A TAMBURA

Chapter 7: Nartana AdhyAya

Saranga Deva discusses how dance originated from Lord Shiva. He defines nAtya as actions that reflect emotions; nritta is body movement alone, and nritya is a combination of both. He broadly classifies body movements in this chapter:

- **The Angas:** head, hands, single-hand poses, combined-hand poses, chest, sides, hips, feet and shoulders.
- **The Pratyangas:** neck, arms, belly and back, thighs, shanks, wrists and knees.
- **The UpAngas:** glances with the eyes, eyebrows, eyelids, pupils, cheeks, nose, breath, lips, teeth, tongue, chin, mouth, heels, ankles, fingers, toes and soles.

When the hands and feet also move with the face to show an emotion or rasa, it's called a karaNa. Saranga lists them out in detail too. If you were to show fear or disgust, how would your hands and feet move? Try that out in front of a mirror!

Watch Yourself

Saranga Deva also gives us a list of the characteristics of a good audience. Are you one?

- People who are fair in their judgement and don't have extreme opinions.
- People who listen well and speak nicely.
- People who know about an ancient Indian way of reasoning called nyAya.
- People who understand good and bad dancing (Saranga Deva lists them).

- People who are humble and not show-offs.
- People who understand feelings and emotions expressed in performances.
- People who are good at understanding music.
- People who can tell when someone isn't speaking correctly.
- People who are smart and don't get jealous.
- People whose hearts are full of appreciation for art.

Multiple karaNas together make an angahAra – literally, a garland of the body parts. Circular motions with the neck, ankles and so on are called rechakas. Charis are movements from the hips to the toes.

He discusses the nine emotions and ends the chapter and the book with a humble request to only take what's good. He admits that there may have been mistakes because nobody's perfect.

He says he was following the path of wise teachers before him when he wrote this and not to brag or boast, and he asks us to like his work because you care for him, in the way the monkeys helped Rama cross the sea because they cared for him.

Finally, he hopes that this book will help you remember him always.

Isn't it amazing how much thought and knowledge goes into the music we enjoy?

11

PAINTING

CHITRA SUTRA

This book is like having an art teacher whispering ancient secrets into your ear – about how to make blue colour from crushed stones, how to paint a person so that they look real enough to step right out of the picture, and how to portray action and adventures using painting.

Ready to discover what artists knew centuries before your great-great-great-(and so on and so forth)-grandparents were even born?

The book is hidden in a secret location.

Chitra means 'to paint' and Sutra means 'the rule'. The *Chitra Sutra* is part of another book called the *Vishnu Dharmottara*, which is itself a part of a bigger book called the *Vishnu Purana*. The *Chitra Sutra* covers only nine chapters within the *Vishnu Dharmottara*. However, they are so detailed, unique and precious that this is considered a separate book.

There are many copies of the book – some even in Nepal and Bangladesh! Even though it was translated and published a century ago, when India was ruled by the British, the book was never studied properly. Gradually its popularity grew as painters in the art world started talking about it. However, there's still a huge gap – many artists and painters don't know about the existence of this treasure trove of knowledge.

WHO WROTE IT AND WHEN?

Sadly, we don't know, but judging by the paintings and sculptures that follow its rules, many believe it's at least 1,000 to 1,500 years old and possibly from Kashmir.

THE BOOK

One day, King Vajra was having a chat with the very wise sage, Markandeya. The king felt quite sad because people couldn't see the divine things in Nature anymore – in the trees, flowers, animals, or even in other people.

'What can we do to help people feel connected to these amazing things again?' asked the king.

The sage Markandeya gave the king the idea to build temples where people could pray and also learn more about themselves. He explained that to build proper temples, people needed to learn six different skills:

1. dancing
2. painting
3. sculpting from stone or wood
4. designing and constructing buildings (architecture)
5. singing and playing musical instruments
6. writing poetry

The wise teacher said that all these skills were equally important – like pieces of a puzzle that work together perfectly.

Markandeya then explained each of these skills clearly. Chapters 35–43 are about painting.

How the First Painting Came to Life

Chapters 35 and 36 teach us the basic measurements needed to draw human beings and gods properly.

The Amazing Story of the Very First Painting

Long, long ago, a wise sage called Narayana in heaven made the very first painting ever!

He squeezed some sap from a mango tree and used it like paint to draw a picture of a woman on his thigh (which is called 'uru' in Sanskrit).

His painting was so incredibly lifelike and perfect that something magical happened: the woman in the painting actually came to life!

She became Urvashi, who was one of the cleverest and most beautiful apsarAs.

The Different Types of People You Can Draw

According to the author, there are five types of humans that artists can draw:

1. Hamsa – swan-like
2. Bhadra – gracious
3. MAlavya – like the people of Malwa

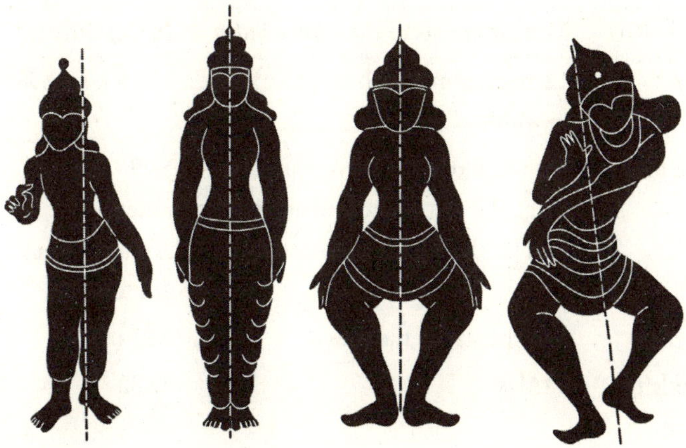

4. Ruchaka – pigeon-like
5. Shashaka – hare-like

How to Measure Drawings

The wise teacher gives us the exact measurements for each type of model using a special unit called 'angula'. One angula is roughly the width of a grown-up's thumb (around 1.763 centimetres). When you put 12 angulas together, you get one 'tAla', while 1 pada is a quarter of a 'tAla'.

For example, if you want to draw a Hamsa type of person, they must be exactly 108 angulas tall. The teacher then explains how to split up these measurements for different parts of the body with exact measurements and proportions. (If you want to learn more about the movements and expressions mentioned here, check out the chapter on the *Natya Shastra*.)

Body parts and their ideal measurements are mentioned in the text. Every detailed proportion is there for everything from tooth to toenail! Here are a few examples:

Body Part	Measurements in the *Chitra Sutra*	In Centimetres
Feet	12 angulas in length and 6 angulas in width.	21.16 L x 10.58 W
The toes	Big toe and index toe – 3 angulas long. The rest of the toes are less by ⅛th [of the big toe progressively].	5.29 – big toe, index; 3rd toe – 4.66; 4th toe – 4.1
Toenail	¼th the size of the toes	0.25 of toe
Ankle to knee	2 tAlas	42.32
Thighs	Same as ankle to knee – 2 tAlas	42.32
Neck	⅓rd of a tAla	6.98
Face	1 tAla	21.16
Palm	1 tAla	21.16
Forearm	17 angulas	29.97
Cheeks	5 angulas	8.82
Jaws	4 angulas in width and 2 angulas in height	7.05 W; 3.53 H
Ears	2 angulas in width and 4 in height	3.53 W; 7.05 H
Ear hole	½ angula	0.88
Nose	4 angulas in length	7.05
Distance between the nose and the upper lip	½ angula	0.88
Upper lip	1 angula in thickness	1.763
Mouth	4 angulas in width	7.05

Lower lip	1 angula	1.763
32 teeth, of which 8 are canines	½ angula in height	0.88
The canines	1½ angula in height	2.64
Eyes	1 angula in width and 3 angulas in length	1.763 W; 5.29 L
Black orb of the eye	⅓rd of the eyes	
Pupil	1/5th of the orb	
Eyebrows	½ an angula in breadth and 4 angulas in length	0.88 B; 7.05 L
Space between the eyebrows	2 angulas	3.53
Distance between the end of the eyes and the ears	4 angulas	7.05
Using such ratios, any figure can be created. For instance, a Bhadra's overall height is 106 angulas, a MAlavya's is 104 angulas, a Ruchaka's is 100 angulas, a Shashaka's is 92 and so on.		Bhadra – 186.88 MAlavya – 183.35 Ruchaka – 176.3 Shashaka – 162.2

The chapter ends with suggestions on features and colours for each type. For example, the Shashaka man should be painted reddish brown or a dark blue/black with slightly protruding teeth, full cheeks and large eyelids. The painting should show that he's a clever person.

How to Draw Gods, Goddesses and Kings

In chapters 37 and 38, the *Chitra Sutra* lists rules for drawing or making statues of gods, goddesses and kings. Gods and goddesses needed to be shown smiling. Artists adorned them with beautiful jewellery and gave them glowing halos.

Kings had to look special too. Their feet needed to be slightly webbed (like a duck's), and they had a small tuft of hair growing between their eyebrows. Artists also gave them halos around their heads and loads of fancy jewellery to show how important they were.

Eye Shapes

The shapes of the eyes were very important and varied depending on the emotions:

- **Fish-belly eyes:** Suitable for women and looked like the rounded tummy of a fish.
- **Lotus-petal eyes:** Used to depict a frightened person or someone who's been crying, and for gods and goddesses. The eyes had to look very kind and stare straight ahead. The old books warned that terrible things would happen if a deity's eyes weren't looking directly forward!
- **Bow-shaped eyes:** These were used when someone was deep in thought or meditating.
- **Cowrie-shell eyes:** These showed someone in pain or someone who's angry.

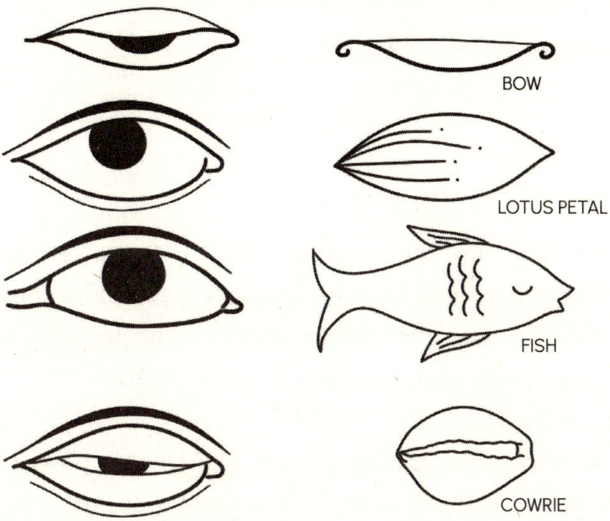

A FEW OF THE DIFFERENT TYPES OF EYE SHAPES DESCRIBED IN THE *CHITRA SUTRA* – ISN'T IT COOL HOW MANY OF THEM WERE BASED ON SHAPES FOUND IN NATURE?

Good Hair Days for the Deities

The ancient artists drew gods and goddesses with gorgeous hair, wavy and silky smooth, shining with natural oils that made the tresses look as sparkly as a beautiful sapphire. Artists could choose from seven different hairstyles:

- locks that hung down neatly (kuntala)
- curls that twisted one way (dakshinAvarta)
- gentle waves (taranga)
- wild hair like a lion's mane (simha-kesara)

- tight curls (barbara)
- twisted hair braided together (jUTaka)
- matted dreadlocks (saTa)

A Pocketful of Poses

Chapter 39 is all about postures. There are four basic ways to paint a person: full face-on, full back-view and right or left profile. There are five other poses where the person is turned slightly – with small variations in the positions of the legs, hips, body, arms, neck and face.

According to the book, the full-frontal pose (facing completely forward) is the best, especially for painting gods and goddesses.

A FULLY FRONT-FACING POSE WAS CONSIDERED THE BEST WHILE PAINTING DEITIES

There are special poses mentioned too:

- Warriors with swords and shields stand in a zigzag position, ready for action.
- People holding spears, arrows or stones should appear to be in motion – walking, working hard or shooting/launching their weapons.
- Anyone carrying discs, long spears, clubs or lances should seem to be leaping around.

Mastering Plaster

Chapter 40 is all about preparing the plaster for murals. You can't paint directly on a rough brick or stone wall, right?

Making the Plaster – The Recipe

- Mix clay with brick dust (in a 1 : 3 ratio).
- Add equal amounts of bdellium tree gum, beeswax, an extract from a plant called *Bassia latifolia* (mahua), an extract from the deodar tree, and jaggery. Mix them all with safflower oil.
- Add a third part of burnt plaster powder to this mixture.
- Mix in two parts of coarse grass and one part of hemp fibres.
- Soak the whole mixture thoroughly in a slimy sugar solution and leave it for exactly one month.

After a month, the plaster becomes soft and malleable, easy to spread on a dry wall to create a smooth surface for painting. When spread, it should be neither too thick nor too thin, and the plasterer must ensure that there are no bumps or dips. Smooth it as soon as it dries by rubbing with a mixture of clay and oil from the plant *Vatica robusta* (ashvakarna). Then smear gently and continuously with milk until the surface becomes perfectly plain.

Follow these steps diligently, and the wall will stay strong and beautiful for hundreds of years without falling apart – and this is indeed true!

When the wall is dry, after reciting prayers on an auspicious day, the artist dons white clothes, sketches everything in white, then brown and finally black paint or chalk, according to the correct proportions and poses. Finally, all the colours are filled in to complete the mural.

The author of the text discusses how to make the colours in the chapter on makeup for dance. He lists the primary colours as white, yellow, red, blue and black. By mixing these in different proportions, you can generate more than 1,000 shades, he says. Colours can also come from metals and minerals like gold, silver, copper, mica, lapis lazuli, ultramarine (rAjAvarta), red lead, tin, yellow orpiment, lime, lac, vermilion and indigo. Use liquid mica and/or the milk of the Sindura tree, so the colours mix and stick to the plaster. Much research obviously went into what would work!

Style File

Chapter 41 deals with four basic types of painting:

- **Satya or Naturalistic:** Looks just like the real world around us.
- **Daishika or Provincial/Local:** Tall, stretched figures that are large, painted effortlessly and decoratively in balanced compositions. These use a plumb line for symmetrical frontal poses.
- **Nagara or Urban/Professional**: Shows 3-D solid figures with mathematical circles to work out perspective and foreshortening, and very little decoration added except for simple garlands.
- **Mishra or Mixed**: Combines all the three types above.

There are also three different ways to draw lines:

- **Patraja** (leaf-like, soft, branching, vein-like lines);
- **Acchaidika** (fine and unbroken); and
- **Binduja** (dot-based lines).

Bad paintings have problems like lines that are too weak or too thick, lack variety, and have oversized eyes/lips/cheeks, inconsistencies and disproportion. Good paintings have proper use of perpendiculars for perfect postures and proportions, loveliness, variety, realism and foreshortening (making things look 3D). The four main elements that make up any painting are the basic lines, how those lines are drawn, the decorations and the colours used.

The chapter ends with a checklist for a good or bad painting – how do yours score?

- Smooth, clear lines
- Beautiful colours

- Appropriate clothing/dress
- Perfect proportions

Remember: The goal is to make a painting so stunning and lifelike that it captivates everyone who looks at it!

Chapter 42 provides a list of rules to portray gods, humans and the seasons.

When drawing pishAchas (goblins), dwarfs and pramatha gaNa (a group of fierce supernatural beings), you don't need to follow the regular guidelines for how bodies should look or what colours to use. You can make their heads too big or too small, their arms very long or very short and paint them in any colours you want, even unnatural ones. The rAkshasas should be made to look terrifying with their hair raised and large eyes. Since these are supernatural beings, you have the freedom to make them look unusual and otherworldly.

When painting military figures, the expert artist should depict the army commander as confident and mighty. The warriors should be tall and towering with frowning faces that reflect their fierce nature. The foot soldiers should be painted to look proud, haughty and battle-ready as they march forwards carrying their weapons. Warriors must always be painted with footwear.

Wrestlers should be depicted as muscular, tall, thick-necked and short-haired.

Mountains must be painted with many rocks, peaks, minerals, trees, waterfalls and snakes.

To depict night-time in a painting, the artist should draw people asleep, a thief sneaking around and things that normally happen at night, along with the moon, planets and stars in the sky. To show dawn or early morning, the artist should paint the sun coming up, lamps growing dim because morning is here and a rooster crowing to announce the new day.

To show summer in a painting, the artist should draw tired people and deer resting in the shade, creatures that look weak and suffering from the sweltering heat of the sun and buffaloes wallowing in mud. The artist should also paint dried-up ponds with little or no water, birds clinging close to trees to find shade, and lions and tigers hiding in caves to escape the heat.

Finally, sage Markandeya says, the painting must be as lifelike as possible, with the correct colours and objects for that time and place. The artist should also convey the emotions he wants viewers to have.

Chapter 43 connects the painting to the emotions it needs to create in the viewer. Nine emotions are mentioned:

- love (sringAra)
- humour (hAsya)
- pathos (karuNa)
- bravery (vIra)
- anger (raudra)
- fright (bhayAnaka)
- disgust (vibhatsa)
- wonder (adbhuta) and
- peace (shAnta)

There are detailed notes for each. For example, if the painting has to portray a heroic emotion, the artist should show the hero taking an oath, displaying pride and performing brave acts. The hero should be painted with a frowning face and a lordly expression to portray strength and courage.

The last few verses provide general rules and another checklist for a good painter, one of the points being that they should be able to illustrate 'movement' – waves, flames, smoke, flags, fluttering garments and so on. While painting a sleeping person, the painter must ensure that the sleeping person doesn't look dead! When painting people who are doing things or looking at the viewer, they must look so real that the viewer actually wants to talk to them.

Sage Markandeya tells King Vajra:

'O King, what you have been taught so far is just a short summary, because it would take hundreds of years to explain all the detailed rules of painting. A house that has paintings in it is considered very lucky and blessed. Just as Sumeru is the greatest mountain and Garuda is the king of all birds, painting is the best and most important of all the arts.'

12

PERFORMING ARTS

NATYA SHASTRA

Did you know that nAtya means more than just dance? It's a mix of dance (nritya), music (gIta) and playing instruments (vAdya). And shAstra means something that teaches you, like a guide. So, the *Natya Shastra* is a book that teaches us how to perform arts like dancing, singing and playing musical instruments.

This incredible book was written by Bharata, who lived a long time ago – maybe between 200 BCE and 200 CE! But we don't know much about Bharata himself because, like many other writers of the time, he did not talk about himself. Today we see dance, music and plays separately. In those days, they were all presented together. In plays, the actors danced, sang and spoke their dialogues.

WHY WAS IT WRITTEN?

A long time ago, it is said, people on Earth were greedy, jealous and bad-tempered. They hurt each other and caused chaos. The wisdom to stop this kind of bad behaviour was in the Vedas, but not everyone could read them. So, Brahma, the creator, made a 'Fifth' Veda – 'Natya Veda' – so that everyone could enjoy them and learn the wisdom of the Vedas. This art of music and dance was a teaching tool to help people live happy lives without greed, envy and anger.

Brahma shared this knowledge with Bharata, who in turn taught it to his 100 sons (or students, who were like his children). They performed plays to spread this wisdom, and the tradition of nAtya began!

INSIDE THE BOOK

This book has 37 chapters that teach everything about the performing arts. Here's what it covers:

A long time ago, a group of sages asked Bharata five questions:

- Why was the *Natya Shastra* created?
- Who can learn it?
- What are its parts?
- How large is it?
- How can it be practised?

The remaining chapters answer these questions, although not in this same order.

- **How to Build a Stage and Start a Performance**: Chapters 2 and 3 explain stage construction and the rituals to begin a show. Different shapes of theatres are mentioned:
  - square,
  - rectangular and
  - triangular

with the rectangular one considered the best for drama.

- **Dancer's Guide**: Chapter 4 lists 108 dance movements, beautifully depicted in the Nataraja temple in Chidambaram in Tamil Nadu.
- **Emotions and Expressions**: Chapters 6 and 7 describe eight emotions (rasas): Love, Humour, Pathos, Anger, Courage, Fear, Disgust and Wonder. Sometime later, Peace was added to this list. These emotions help performers connect with their audience.

This is also the most important contribution of Bharata. These emotions determine the movement of the body, the music and the dialogues. The success of a performance is when the audience feels the emotion with the same intensity as the performer expresses it on stage.

Rules for Good Writing

Bharata also teaches how to write good stories, poems or plays. Here are 10 mistakes to avoid, mentioned in chapter 16 of his book:

1. Using a complicated word that is not normally used instead of using a simpler word, for example, saying, 'He was obdurate', instead of saying, 'he was stubborn'. FYI – Bharata doesn't give examples but only names and explains them.
2. Describing something in a contradictory (or opposite) way.
3. Something that is not logical or unclear and needs someone to explain it.
4. Leaving something incomplete.

5. Using bad words or crude language.
6. Mixing unrelated ideas.
7. Faulty grammar or breaking the rules of writing.
8. When the metre is faulty ('metre' in poetry is like the beat or rhythm in music).
9. Joining words that shouldn't be joined together.
10. Words that have mismatched sounds; good writing must be interesting, easy to read and pleasing to hear.

Fun Facts from Other Chapters

- **Body Movements**: Chapters 8–12 explain how to move your head, hands, eyes and even your eyebrows to express emotions. These chapters have been greatly admired for the logical way in which Bharata wrote them. First, he lists the various movements of each body part. Then he tells us to which rasa they apply.
- **Up on Stage:** Chapter 13 deals with movements on the stage for both plays and dances.
- **Dialogues and Poetry**: Dialogues in those days were usually poetry that was sung rather than spoken. Chapter 14 is about letters, alphabets and their sounds (phonetics). Chapters 15–16 talk about the basic rules poets need to follow. Chapter 17 deals with languages and pronunciation. Some verses are also about how body movements synchronize with the words used.
- **Drama and Happy Endings**: Indian dramas always had happy endings! Death was never shown on stage.

What Makes a Great Teacher?

In Chapter 26, Bharata says a teacher must:

- Be great at singing, dancing and playing instruments, and be able to train others as well.
- Keep a steady beat and a good sense of rhythm.
- Have a good memory, and be smart and intelligent.
- Be creative and ready to unlearn old ideas.

Chapters 18–20 deal with the different types of drama and their sequence. This is the world's first-known text on drama.

Writing a Play or Story: A Cool Lesson

In chapter 19, Bharata explains how every story has five stages:

1. The hero or heroine (protagonist) prepares to achieve something big.
2. They work hard to make it happen.
3. They see hope that success is near.
4. They feel that victory is within reach.
5. They finally achieve it!

Try writing your own story using these stages.

Which of the eight rasas can you bring in each stage?

For that rasa, how will the actor move and speak?

Can you now see how easy Bharata makes writing a play or story?

- **Costumes and Props**: Chapter 21 details costumes, makeup and how props should be light so that actors don't get tired. Bharata says, for example, don't use iron props which are very heavy!
- **Advice for Directors (and Audiences)**: Chapters 22–24 deal with various types of characters and how they can be embellished – their costumes, postures, speech and so on. Chapter 25 deals with various gestures to portray emotions and seasons (e.g., clapping hands over the ears, to show alarm or fear) or gently waving hands (to represent flowers blooming in Spring). Chapter 26 deals with makeup. Chapter 27 deals with what goes into making a play a success, the qualities of an audience, difficulties that can arise while staging a performance, who is qualified to judge a performance and also how it should be judged.
- **Music and Instruments**: Chapters 28–34 cover everything about musical instruments, notes and how to match music with emotions. Chapter 34 is just about drums, of which the three main types are the mridanga, the paNava and the dardura – perhaps those were Bharata's favourites.
- **More Advice for Directors**: Chapter 35 is about assigning the right actors to the right roles. A good actor, according to Bharata, must be able to move gracefully, speak clearly, radiate energy and behave properly. If your character is an ascetic doing severe penance or is a sanyAsi who lives in the forest and eats sparingly, give that role to a skinny person and not to a plump actor, says Bharata. Otherwise, the audience will get very confused!

And what do you get in the end? Chapters 36 and 37 reveal Bharata's secret of nAtya. By following his rules right from

the start, both performers and audiences will live happily – no sadness or anger or fear.

And a good student? Is someone who is intelligent, has a strong memory, can recognize and appreciate good qualities in others, is keen to learn, is competitive and has lots of energy.

Makeup Magic

What do you think the ancient theatre people used for makeup? Here's a surprising list:

White – from chalk, lime, conch shell powder or clay.
To denote purity, gods, sages and calm characters.

Red – from red minerals, red clay, flowers or lac.
Shows bravery, anger, love or heroism.

Black – from lamp soot or burnt oil.
Used for demons, villains, night scenes or strong emotions.

Yellow – from turmeric or yellow earth.
Shows energy, royalty or divine glow.

Green – from leaves, plants or mixed pigments.
Used for Nature spirits or gentle characters.

Blue – from indigo plants or dark minerals.
Connected to gods or mystery or deep emotions.

So, what do you think? Will Bharata consider you a good enough student to teach you the *Natya Shastra*?

This magical book, *Natya Shastra*, isn't just about performing arts – it's about living happily and spreading joy.

Next time you watch a play, a dance, or a movie, remember Bharata's teachings – try to spot how:

- the plot builds up;
- emotions are written into the plot;
- the music, dialogue and body movements demonstrate those emotions.

Enjoy!

13

PLANTS AND TREES

VRIKSHA AYURVEDA

In the eastern corner of India is a wonderfully green state called West Bengal. Up in the northern part of West Bengal is a place with a poetic-sounding name: Cooch Behar. Do you know what that means?

The 'Cooch' or 'Koch' are a tribe of nomadic people who live nearby in Assam, Meghalaya and Bangladesh – 'Behar' is derived from the Sanskrit word 'vihAra', which means 'to roam' or 'to wander around'. So, traditionally, Cooch Behar means 'the land where the Koch people roam'!

Long, long ago – even before your great-great-great-grandparents were born – this place was a kingdom with kings and queens! The Koch kings ruled here from the 13th century (that's about 800 years ago). The city where the king lived still has a beautiful palace today. These kings loved clever people and helped many scholars study, learn and write books. Many, many years later, sometime before 1928, a man named Jogendranath Sircar was rummaging through old books in a library and found a very special manuscript on palm leaves! But oh no! Some of the palm leaves were damaged, and the ending was missing!

Jogendranath thought the book was important, so he made a copy of it. Then his son and granddaughter worked very hard to turn it into a proper book so everyone could read this special story. Coming from such a lush and green region, the book was about plants, what else!

THE BOOK

Did you know that only ONE manuscript of this amazing old book still exists, but no one knows where it is now. Even that is only a replica of the original, lost long ago! This was also incomplete, which is why we don't know the author's name.

Learned experts who study old books have looked at the words used, the sentence structures (sUtras) and the way the information is arranged. They think this book is from around 300–400 CE, which makes it almost 2,000 years old! That's older than your great-great-great-great-great-great-great-great-grandparents (and even more 'greats')!

Other old books, like the *Arthashastra*, mention 'Vriksha Ayurveda' books about trees and plants. Experts say that the very best botany book was written by Parashara. This manuscript might be the only example of his work still around today!

Did you know there are two other books with exactly the same name? They were written by people called Surapala and Sharangadhara. But this one – our mysterious book – even while incomplete, has the most information.

INSIDE THE BOOK

Now let's dive in! Maybe you should sit under a tree or near a plant?

Part 1: BijotpattikAnda – Seeds and Stuff

In a beautiful forest called Chaitraratha, a wise teacher named Parashara sat with his students. He taught them amazing secrets about plants and how they came to exist.

How Life Began

Do you know how the very first plant came to be? According to this book, it began when water turned thick and wobbly like jelly! The sun's warmth and other special energies made this into what we call the 'Adi bIjam' – the very first seed!

From this magic seed, a tiny root sprouted with the help of moisture. Then came the stem, pretty leaves, colourful flowers and tasty fruits!

Types of Plants

Vriksha Ayurveda says that plants have feelings just like you and me. Plants belong to four special groups:

1. Some plants live for a short time, make fruits and then say goodbye. We call them 'annuals' today.
2. Some plants have flowers that like to play hide-and-seek – they're good at hiding! Grasses, for instance.
3. Some plants love to climb and reach for the sky using special curly arms called tendrils. They are called climbers!
4. Some plants stay small, with short branches and roots, and don't have climbing arms.

Lands Where Plants Live

Plants live in three different kinds of lands:

1. **Jangala Land**: This is a very dry place, almost like a desert! The soil has lots of tiny stones and sand. Only the hardiest plants can live here.
2. **Anupa Land**: This is a splashy place with lots of rivers and ponds! It's often near the sea, and the soil feels like clay. The air feels wet when you breathe. The Sunderbans mangrove forest in West Bengal is like this.
3. **Mishra Land**: It's a mix of both wet and dry lands. The soil can be grey, red or black and is great for growing all sorts of plants and trees.

Isn't it amazing how plants find homes in so many different places? They also grow in rocky areas and inhospitable places where only grasses grow!

Greendom

What's your favourite plant?

Do you think it prefers the dry Jangala Land, the wet Anupa Land, or the mixed Mishra Land?

All about Forests

The author then describes the forests of each region of the Indian subcontinent. His vast knowledge is impressive, especially when it was so tough to travel 2,000 years ago! The map of forests based on his descriptions looks like this:

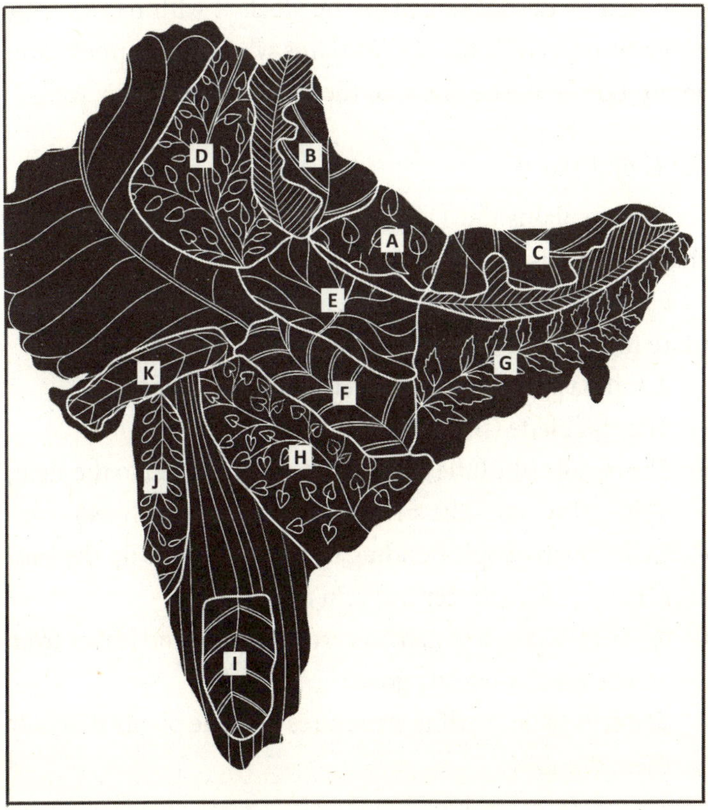

A REIMAGINED MAP OF FORESTS BASED ON THE DETAILS GIVEN IN THE *VRIKSHA AYURVEDA*

- **A** Chaitraratha Vana
- **B** KAlaka Vana
- **C** KirATa Vana
- **D** PAnchanada Vana
- **E** PrAchya Vana
- **F** VedikArushaka Vana
- **G** Angireya Vana
- **H** KAlingaka Vana
- **I** dAshArNaka Vana
- **J** apArAnta Vana
- **K** SaurAshtra Vana

When he describes a plant, he labels it with names from different parts of India and explains why those names came about. Looks like he knew all the Indian forests very well.

Parts of a Plant

He then explains the 11 parts of the plant in the remaining chapters in this section.

Parashara mentions 47 different shapes of leaves. That's more than all your fingers and toes put together!

A leaf has 10 special parts! Here are some of them:

- The leaf blade (the flat part)
- The petiole (the little stalk that attaches the leaf to the stem)
- Veins (tiny tube-like structures that look like lines)
- Cells (microscopic building blocks that make up the leaf)
- Midrib (the main central vein of the leaf)
- Rachis (the central stalk in certain compound leaves from which smaller leaflets grow)
- Tendrils (thin, curling structures in some plants that help them climb)

Turn a New Leaf

Pick up a few fallen leaves and try to spot these parts like a plant detective!

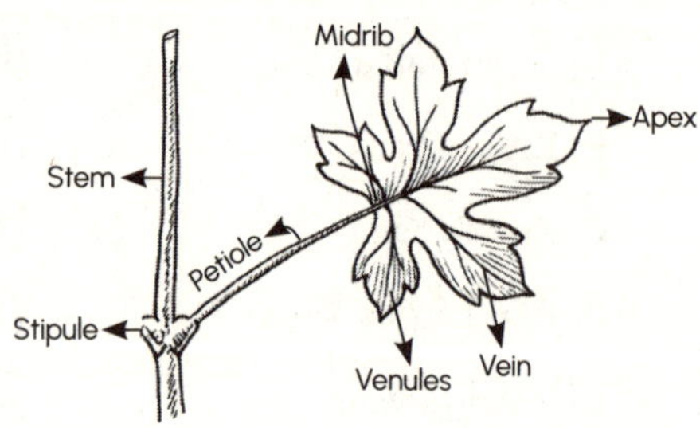

- Leaf sheath (the part that wraps around or hugs the stem; seen in some plants like grasses)
- Leaf apex (the tip of the leaf)

The petiole is extra-special – it can grow in seven different ways depending on where it sits. This teacher was really good at spotting even the tiniest details!

Plant Secrets

Some trees, like the peepul, have a special protective cover called a 'sangam' that keeps new leaves and flower buds safe. It's like a little raincoat for baby leaves!

And of course you know that some flowers only bloom in sunlight – and others in moonlight? Some flowers can make fruits; others can't.

Fruits come in more than nine different types based on shape, seed arrangement and juiciness.

The Most Important Part

Do you know what the plant's most important part is? The roots! They act like the plant's mouth, sipping water from the soil. The roots and bark team up to move the nutrients to all the other parts of the plant.

This wise teacher watched very carefully as seeds split open to sprout tiny roots and shoots – he noted down every tiny detail!

He was excellent at explaining things in the right order – somewhat like beginning with an introduction to the topic of his lecture before his talk, and then summarizing what he said at the end of his lecture.

You'll be amazed at this plant explorer's keen eye for detail. He could see things that most people miss – like how a baby leaf has its own little coat or how there are so many different kinds of leaf shapes!

Part 2: Vanaspati KAnda

Some plants have flowers that are experts at playing hide-and-seek – they're so good at hiding! These flowers stay hidden from both the sun and the moon; they ooze a sticky sap called latex. The hollow fruits grow directly from the stem or the leaf bases. Their seeds split into two parts (dicotyledonous). Their wood is hard enough to use as fuel.

This family – including the banyan tree – has subdivisions based on the leaf shape and arrangement, and the colour of the latex. Even grass-like plants with parallel leaf veins belong to this group; they've been described in detail.

Part 3: Vanaspatya KAnda

These are plants with visible flowers that bear fruits. They include India's top favourite – the mango! Cuckoos love these fruits. The flowers bloom in spring, fragrant enough to attract wasp-like insects. Parashara also praised the jingan (now scientifically known as *Lannea coromandelica*) – its sap can be used as gum.

Many citrus fruits and the jAmun tree are described here, along with leguminous plants such as beans, peas, lentils and peanuts.

This section also describes many plants of the kandula family – their sap causes itching when touched.

One chapter called 'Vriddha Valli Kanda' has plants with only one leaf and a fibrous stem, but no one can figure out what these are!

As if to deepen the mystery, the text ends abruptly here – hopefully someday we'll find the rest.

Other Information in Samhitas

In Sanskrit book lists, you'll often find the word 'Samhita'. This means a collection. Anybody could create a Samhita by copying books or parts of books on diverse subjects on to palm leaves. Bound together it would become a Samhita.

Sharangadhara Samhita, by Sharangadhara (minister 900 years ago to King Hammira of Shakhambari Desha – now in the Bundelkhand in western India), includes 'Vriksha Ayurveda'. Here are some notes from this text to show a different book on the same subject:

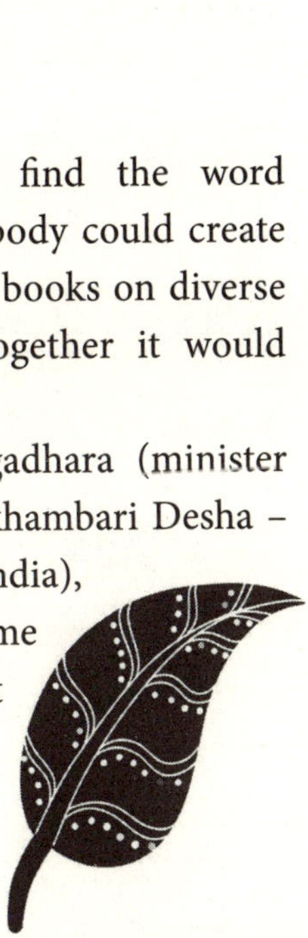

a The first 23 verses praise the benefits of planting trees. Planting one tree that provides rest and shade by the roadside is the greatest good deed one can do – it's like rearing many children to be good human beings!

- Soil can be split into six categories, based on colour and taste.
- The text provides lots of information on how to plant seeds and look after the seedlings: some seeds are to be planted on the surface of the soil, and others beneath the soil. The Samhita says we should water plants depending on the daily weather and soil content – most plants don't like to be in wet soil all the time.

There are many other 'Vriksha Ayurveda' texts – enough to tell us how people back then loved and cared for plants and trees.

14

WRESTLING

MALLA PURANA

Fitness has always been a thing. Today, we play sports like football or cricket or go to the gym to stay fit. But did you know that in ancient times, wrestling was very popular? They even had exciting competitions (kind of like the IPL!).

Wrestling is still popular today – it's even an Olympic sport! But not many know about India's special wrestling tradition. That's why the *Malla Purana* is so important.

Fun Fact

Have you heard of the seaside town called Mahabalipuram near Chennai in Tamil Nadu?

It has many beautiful rock temples. The correct name for the town is Mamalla Puram.

'Ma Malla' means 'great wrestler' – a title for Narasimhavarman I, a Pallava king who lived 1,400 years ago!

THE BOOK

Do you know about the Jyeshti Mallas, the professional wrestlers from Gujarat?

As recently as 50 years ago, these amazing athletes could be found all over India. These days, many have moved on to other jobs, but their story is still exciting!

Delmal is a village near Modhera in Gujarat. It has a temple for Limbaja Mata and an ancient gym. This is the main temple that Jyeshti wrestlers worship at.

The *Malla Purana* is like their history book. It tells us how these wrestlers came to be and shares tons of interesting wrestling facts.

'Malla' isn't just one type of wrestling. It includes wrestling with bare hands, wrestling with a small weapon called a 'vajra', which covers your knuckles (somewhat like a knuckleduster), and even boxing!

There are two versions of this book. One of them is from 1674 CE – that's more than 350 years old! The other book was published in 1911. The first version is missing many chapters, but the second one is more complete. Both of these books are copies, of course. The original book was written sometime between the 15th and 17th centuries.

Both books have lots of Gujarati words mixed with Sanskrit, which tells us that this Purana was originally created in Gujarat.

Who wrote the 18 chapters? Nobody knows! The 1674 work was copied by someone named Dumchandra, but we don't know anything else about him.

INSIDE THE BOOK

The *Malla Puraṇa* explains how mallas (wrestlers) trained, lived, ate and competed in ancient India – like a complete guidebook to becoming strong and skilful in wrestling.

Chapters 1 and 2: The Background Story

The book starts with an introduction to great wrestling events. In the Mahabharata, there was a famous wrestling match. Bhima, one of the heroes, defeated the villain, Duryodhana, in a wrestling match. Krishna, who was very clever, helped guide Bhima to win.

In another instance, two brothers called Balarama and Krishna defeated a cruel king called Kamsa in a wrestling match. After winning, they travelled back to their home, Dwarka, which is in Gujarat. On their way home, King Someshwara, from a place called Mayuravambalam, welcomed them warmly. Mayuravambalam is what we now call Delmal. King Someshwara was such a good king and treated his guests so well that Krishna decided to teach him everything about wrestling.

Chapter 3: Categories and Training

This chapter talks about who was allowed to learn wrestling in ancient times, and focuses on the classification and training of wrestlers. Lord Krishna begins the chapter by preparing for training and delivering a discourse on who is fit to be trained. He classifies the mallas into four categories:

- **Jyeshti**: They are smart and humble (therefore, ready to learn and correct themselves). They eat healthily, they don't hesitate to take on challenges even if they're difficult and are patient enough to overcome hurdles in order to win. They were the highest-ranked senior champions – usually undefeated or legendary – and were attached to royal courts. They performed in state festivals, coronations and ceremonial bouts. They were masters of akhARas (wrestling arenas) and trained other wrestlers.
- **Antarajyeshti**: These were the second rung of elite palace wrestlers who participated in bouts against other top-ranked opponents.
- **Gopakula**: These wrestlers came from pastoral or cowherd groups, following in the footsteps of Krishna, who is also described as a powerful wrestler. They practised in village akhARas and focused on strength-based wrestling.
- **Bhavishya**: These were 'future' or upcoming trainees and novices, expected to rise to higher ranks after being fully groomed in akhARas.

Each group is described in terms of how they think and behave, and their physical strength.

Chapter 4: The Qualities of Wrestlers

All wrestlers must have special qualities related to their bodies and minds! Based on the structure of their body, there are five types:

- *Asthishara* – dominated by bone.
- *MAmsashara* – dominated by muscle.
- *Medashara* – dominated by bone marrow.
- *Asthi-MAmsashara* – combination of bone and muscle.
- *Medasthishara* – combination of fat and bone.

Here, too, different grades and classifications are discussed. The worst grade includes those who may have a strong body but aren't humble; are cowardly; are all talk and no action; and those who don't think logically. Don't you think these factors are relevant even now?

Chapters 5, 15, 16 and 17: Types of Wrestlers

These chapters describe different kinds of wrestlers and deal with which type of wrestling suits which kind of people. They use different ways to categorize wrestlers:

- The strongest wrestlers were called 'jyeshti'. Their 'seconds', who weren't quite as strong, were called 'antarjyeshti' as mentioned earlier.

- Wrestlers were also grouped by age.
- They were grouped by how strong different parts of their bodies were, such as the chest, arms, waist, shoulders and knees.

Chapter 6: Training and Wrestling Gyms

This chapter explains how wrestlers should train and what a proper wrestling gym (called an 'akhARaka') should be. They have to focus on different parts of their bodies and strengthen them: urushara (thigh strength), skandhashara (shoulder strength), bhujAshara (arm strength), kaTishara (waist strength) and jAnushara (knee strength).

The ranga-bhUmi or wrestling arena (akhARaka) is then described, noting its three forms – low, level and high – and its dimensions. These are measured in hastas (1 hasta = 1.5 feet long):

- 101 hastas: the best size – even the gods use this.
- 50 hastas: this is average – asuras use this.
- 21 hastas: the size used for human beings.

Stages can be shaped like a square, a triangle or a circle. The ideal soil colours and cleanliness (specifically the removal of harmful materials like thorns, wood and iron) are emphasized.

Next, the wrestler or malla's daily routine is described. He has to wake up early, brush his teeth, perform prayers, do breathing exercises (prANAyAma), pray to Earth and complete a warm-up (yes, stretching exercises). He is warned against wasting time on the wrong kind of people or behaviour.

After he worships various gods such as Krishna, Haladhara and Vasuki, he tightens his loincloth, beats his arms and shoulders with his palms, prays to and seeks forgiveness from Mother Earth, takes a little soil from the arena and smears it on his body – and *then* starts practising or wrestling while listening to the instructions of the teacher, called the matilAra.

Chapter 7: Wrestling Sounds and Moves

This chapter talks about what wrestlers should not say or do: such as insult or taunt an opponent. It also describes many special hand grips and movements called 'ghaTas'. Several throwing techniques are mentioned too, but the exact meanings of these ancient words are too hard for us to understand today.

Chapters 8 and 12: Daily Routines for Wrestlers

These chapters explain what wrestlers should do every day:

- Wake up at the crack of dawn;
- Bathe in cold water;
- Drink plenty of milk;
- Eat fresh grapes (considered 'athlete fuel' at the time!); and
- Follow a strictly regulated diet.

Chapters 9, 10 and 11: Wrestling Exercises

These chapters describe all the exercises wrestlers were required to do. Some wrestlers wore special weapons on their fingers, like the vajra-mushTi. Usually, wrestling mainly involved the arms, but wrestlers were also permitted to:

- Kick;
- Press with the knee; and
- Hit on the head or face.

However, hitting below the chest was against the rules.

A wrestler lost if:

- He was pinned to the ground;
- His finger weapon broke; or
- He was forced onto his back.

Importantly, wrestlers weren't allowed to be killed during a match. If a wrestler died, the king was held responsible for the death. The match ended as soon as someone fell to the ground.

The vajra-mushTis they wielded, wearing them on their hands, looked like these:

Chapters 13 and 14: Wrestling Contests

These chapters explain how to organize wrestling competitions and how to win them. Kings arranged these bouts as entertainment for the people. The special stage where wrestling matches took place was called a 'ranga mandapa'.

Types of Wrestling Exercises

- **SthambAshrama Exercises**: These exercises were done using a smooth wooden pillar fixed to the ground or suspended from the ceiling.
- **Mallasthamba Exercises**: These were exercises done with a wooden club. These exercises are once again becoming popular today! They help to build great upper body strength.
- **Exercises for Knees**: These special exercises were specifically designed to make the knees stronger.
- **GoNitA and NAli Exercises:** 'GoNitA' must've been a very popular piece of equipment because numerous exercises involving this are mentioned. It was probably a training object (like modern-day weights) used in wrestling practice. 'NAli' are stone rings with a handle in the middle. They help strengthen the shoulders.
- **Other Important Exercises**: Swimming was essential for developing a strong chest. Climbing up and down ladders was also a good exercise. Circular movements like cartwheels were important when using the vajra-mushTi. Walking and skipping were also key exercises.
- **Mental Exercise**: 'UhApohAshrama' was a special exercise just for the mind! It was all about strategic thinking and planning ahead how to fight and win. This is what coaches help sportspeople do now, isn't it?

- **Massage (mardana):** Massage was considered very important. Different types of massage are mentioned, including special techniques for young children.
- **Partner Exercises**: Some exercises needed to be done with a partner.

The *Malla Purana* warns that you should NOT exercise when you're tired, hungry, scared, anxious, or feeling weak or ill. You should exercise in the morning and take one day of rest every week.

Chapter 18: Winding Up

In the last chapter, there's a summary of 'Malla Shastra' (the science of wrestling). It speaks of of King Someshwara seeking Lord Krishna's protection; in response, Krishna creates a goddess called Limbaja Devi, the guardian of all wrestlers of the Jyeshthi Malla clan. The book concludes by talking about 12 special families of wrestlers and outlining the code of conduct that every wrestler must follow.

Even today, in the Limbaji Mata temple in Delmal, at the conclusion of the evening puja, this unique tradition continues:

- the Jyeshtimallas perform a silent ritual;
- they quickly pat their shoulders with their palms; and
- whisper a prayer in Gujarati for the goddess to bestow them with strength.

It is a powerful reminder that the ancient spirit of the *Malla Purana* is a living practice that continues to this day.

Malla Moves

Wrestling has many exercises and several types of moves – can you invent some moves inspired by animals?

- Tiger stretch?
- Monkey balance?
- Turtle slow walk?
- Crane pose?

Name each move and decide when to use it and why it helps.

THE BIG STUFF IN THIS BOOK

We read about 14 super-old books written in Sanskrit. Together, they have around 9,500 pages – that's like reading all your schoolbooks many times over! Here's what we discovered:

1. Sanskrit Was Like the Internet of Smart People Long Ago

- Educated people from all over India used Sanskrit to write down their best ideas. There would've been millions of people who didn't know Sanskrit but possessed just as much knowledge from it being passed down orally.
- Sanskrit formed a common thread among certain types of scholars across the different regions of India.
- Even though the texts started with a little prayer, they weren't really about religion – they were about learning stuff.

2. Everything is Connected to Everything Else

- All the authors believed that everything in the world is interconnected, like a gigantic invisible web.
- They wrote about how our feelings connect to:
  - Art and music;
  - Trees, animals and Nature;
  - How we think; and
  - Even things like money and business.

They believed you can't just learn one thing – all the various subjects and topics are interlinked in some way.

⊕•⊕•⊕

3. These Writers Were Very Organized

- Every single book was written really clearly and neatly. It wouldn't have been easy to simply erase or 'delete' mistakes – can you imagine the effort they must've made to get it just right?
- The writers were great at picking the right stuff to say and composing it as poems, so that it could be memorized easily and passed down over centuries.
- The content was put in the right order (with headings and sections).
- They never wasted words – everything they wrote was important for the topic.
- They were honest. Many books actually say upfront that the writer is only compiling existing information.

⊕•⊕•⊕

4. They Asked Big Questions About Life

Even when writing about mathematics or science, these authors asked deep questions like:

- What makes people happy?
- What's the point of life?
- How can knowledge help us?

⊕•⊕•⊕

5. The People Who Saved These Books for Us

- These books were written on fragile palm leaves that became brittle over hundreds of years. Knowledge-seeking and meticulous librarians and book lovers carefully preserved these delicate manuscripts, even as they were crumbling.

Then came the other heroes – the translators who spent their whole lives working on these books:

- They had to piece together incomplete manuscripts like solving ginormous puzzles.
- They had to read tiny, faded letters on the crumbling palm leaves.
- Many of them didn't have much money, but spent years and years on this work anyway, figuring out the difficult technical words and reading tons of other books to help clarify the original text.

Thanks to these dedicated people, all 14 books are now available online for FREE. You see, over time, things – including knowledge – may be lost. Writers may be long gone. But somehow time – and people – have a way of finding everything that matters.

SAY IT RIGHT!

THE OFFICIAL (SORT OF) PRONUNCIATION GUIDE

The list below will help you in two ways:
(1) It will help you pronounce correctly the Sanskrit and Hindi names of people and books/texts mentioned in this book, which are written as they are usually written in English, and
(2) It will help you understand what the weird capital letters in the middle of certain words in the book mean, and how to pronounce those words correctly. Try it and see!

a – a as in **al**ong
A – aa as in f**ar**
ch – ch as in **ch**ain
cH – aspirated ch (छ)
d – soft d as in **th**em
D – hard d, as in **d**og
dri – soft dri (ह)
dh – aspirated soft d (ध)
Dh – aspirated hard d (ढ)
eY – ay as in p**ay**
g – g as in **g**ame
h – soft exhalation through mouth. As in tapa**h**, written in Sanskrit as**:**
i – i as in tr**i**p
I – ee as in tr**ee**
jn – nasal gn sound (ज्ञ)
kh – aspirated k (ख)
n – soft n as in **n**ame
N – hard n (ण)
O – long oh, as in **o**nus

R – quick D, where the tongue curls slightly back and taps the roof of the mouth once (ड़)

Sha – harder sha with tongue curled back (ष)

t – soft t as in pas**ta** (त)

T – hard T as in **t**ell (ट)

th – aspirated soft t, as in **th**under (थ)

Th – aspirated hard t (ठ)

u – u as in f**u**ll

U – oo as in gr**oo**m

⊕•⊕•⊕

Word	**How to Say It**
Acharya Rasa Vagbhata	AchArya Rasa VAgbhaTa
Adhyaya	adhyAya
Agrahayana	agrahAyana
Arthashastra	ArthashAstra
Aryabhata	AryabhaTa
Aryabhatiya	AryabhaTiya
Ashtadhyayi	ashTadhyAyi
Balarama	balarAma
Bhaskaracharya	bhAskarAchArya
Bhima	bhIma
Brahmi	brAhmI
Chitra Sutra	chitra sUtra
Devanagari	devanAgarI
Dumchandra	dumchandra
Haladhara	halAdhara
Jyeshti Malla	jyeshThi malla
Kalyani Chalukya	kalyANi chAlukya
Kartika Sankranti	kArtika sankrAnti
Kautilya	kauTilya
Krishi Parashara	krishi parAshara
Krishna	krishNa
Lilavati	lIlAvatI

Limbaja Devi	limbajA devI
Mahabhashya	mahAbhAshya
Malla Purana	malla purANa
Manasollasa	mAnasOllAsa
Marichi Samhita	mArIchi samhitA
Markandeya	mArkanDeya
Mayuravamblam	mayUravAmbalam
Panini	pANini
Parashara	ParAshara
Prajapati	prajApati
Purana	purANa
Rasaratnakara	rasaratnAkara
Rudrapatna Shamasastry	rudrapatNa shAmashAstri
Samhita	samhitA
Sangita Ratnakara	sangIta ratnAkara
Saranga Deva	sAranga deva
Sharangadhara	ShArangadhara
Shulba Sutra	shulba sUtra
Siddhanta Shiromani	SiddhAnta ShirOmaNi
Sindura	SindUra
Someshvara/Someshwara	sOmeshvara
Surapala	SurapAla
Swastika	swAstika
Vasantaraja Shakuna	vasantrAj shakuna
Vasuki	vAsuki
Vayu	vAyu
Vishnu Dharmottara	vishnu dharmOttara

PS: *If certain Sanskrit/Hindi words in the book aren't included here, it means that they have to be pronounced just as they are written, following the Pronunciation Guide.*

SELECT BIBLIOGRAPHY AND FURTHER READING

If you're curious to explore more about Sanskrit and its incredible history, here are some excellent books and resources:

Burrow, T., *The Sanskrit Language*, Motilal Banarsidass Publishers Pvt. Ltd., 1955

______ A classic scholarly introduction to the structure and development of Sanskrit.

Mishra, Sampadananda, and Vijay, *The Wonder That Is Sanskrit*, Auro Publications, Sri Aurobindo Society, 2002

______ A beautifully written and accessible book that highlights the unique charm and depth of Sanskrit.

Pollock, Sheldon, *The Language of the Gods in the World of Men: Sanskrit, Culture, and Power in Premodern India*, University of California Press, 2006

______ A powerful and in-depth look at how Sanskrit shaped politics, power and culture across Indian history.

Varadachari, V., *A History of the Samskrta Literature*, Kuppuswami Sastri Research Institute, 2014

______ A comprehensive overview of Sanskrit literature, its evolution and its many genres.

Official Sanskrit Portal (Govt. of India): https://www.sanskrit.nic.in/index.php

______ A great resource for Sanskrit learners, teachers and enthusiasts, with books, links and language tools.

ARTHASHASTRA

Shamasastry, R., Kautilya's *Arthashastra*, Translated into English, Government Press, Bangalore, 1915.

ARYABHATIYA

Shukla, Kripa Shankar, K.V. Sarma, *Aryabhatiya of Aryabhata*: Critically Edited with Introduction, English Translation, Notes, Comments and Indexes, Indian National Science Academy, 1976.

CHARAKA SAMHITA

Sharma, Priyavrat, *Charaka Samhita: Agnivesha's Treatise Refined and Annotated by Charaka and Redacted by Dridhabhala* (Text with English Translation), Vol. 1., Varanasi: Chaukambha Orientalia, 1981.

Sharma, P.V., *Charaka Samhita* (Text with English Translation), Vol. 2., Varanasi: Chaukambha Orientalia, 1998.

CHITRA SUTRA

Mukherji, Parul Dave. *The Chitrasutra of the Visnudharmottara Purana*. Motilal Banarsidass Publishers Pvt. Ltd., 2001.

Shah, Priyabala. *Visnudharmottara Purana: A Text on Ancient Indian Arts*. The New Order Book Co., 1990.

KRISHI PARASHARA

Majumdar, Girija Prasanna, and Sures Chandra Banerji, editors and translators. *Krsi-Parasara.* The Asiatic Society, 1960. Bibliotheca Indica: A Collection of Oriental Works, work no. 285, issue no. 1579.

LILAVATI

Patwardhan, K.S., Somashekhara, A.N. and Shyam, L.S., *Lilavati of Bhaskaracharya: A Treatise of Mathematics of Vedic Tradition*, Motilal Banarsidass Publishers, 2001.

MALLA PURANA

Sandesara, B.J. and Mehta, R.N. (eds.), *Mallapurāṇa: A Rare Sanskrit Text on Indian Wrestling Especially as Practised by the Jyesthimallas*, Oriental Institute, Baroda, 1964.

MANASOLLASA

Someshvara, King Bhulokamalla. *Manasollasa.* Vol. 1. Edited by G.K. Shrigondekar, Oriental Institute, 1967. Gaekwad's Oriental Series, no. 28.

Someshvara, King. *Manasollasa.* Vol. 2. Edited with an introduction by G.K. Shrigondekar, Oriental Institute, 1939. Gaekwad's Oriental Series, no. 84.

Someshvara, King. *Manasollasa.* Vol. 3. Edited by G.K. Shrigondekar, Oriental Institute, 1961. Gaekwad's Oriental Series, no. 138.

MAYAMATA

Dagens, Bruno, *Mayamata - Treatise on Housing, Architecture and Iconography*, Sanskrit text edited and translated by Bruno Dagens, Volumes I and II, The Kalamulasutra Series - Part 14, Indira Gandhi National Centre for the Arts and Motilal Banarsidass Publishers, New Delhi, 2007.

NATYA SHASTRA

Rao, Venugopala P, *Natyasastra with Samsodhini Vyakhya*, Volumes 1, 2, 3, Indica Classical Library, Hyderabad, 2024.

RASARATNA-SAMUCCHAYA

Shankar Lal Hari Shankar, *Rasa Ratna Samucchaya of Vagbhatacharya*, Khemraj Shrikrishnadass, 2019.

SANGITA RATNAKARA

Sarngadeva: Sangita-Ratnakara, Sanskrit Text and English Translation with Comments and Notes, Vol. I, Treatment of Svara, Translated by R.K. Shringy, Supervised by P.L. Sharma, Delhi: Motilal Banarsidass, 1978.

Sarngadeva: Sangita-Ratnakara, Sanskrit Text and English Translation with Comments and Notes, Vol. II, Chapters II–IV, Translated by R.K. Shringy, Supervised by P.L. Sharma, New Delhi: Munshiram Manoharlal Publishers Pvt. Ltd., 1989.

Raja, K. Kunjunni and Radha Burnier, trans. *Sangitaratnakara of Sarngadeva*, Vol. IV, Chapter on Dancing, The Adyar Library and Research Centre, Adyar, Madras, 1976.

Subrahmanya Sastri, S., ed., revised by Sarada, S. *Samgitaratnakara of Sarngadeva, with the Kalanidhi of Kallinatha and the Sudhakara of Simhabhupala*, Vol. III, Adhyaya 5 and 6. The Adyar Library and Research Centre, Madras, 1986.

SUSHRUTA SAMHITA

Bhishagratna, K.L. (Ed.), *An English translation of the Sushruta Samhita based on original Sanskrit text* (Vol. 1), No. 10, Kashi Ghose's Lane, Calcutta, 1907.

Bhishagratna, K.L. (Ed.), *An English translation of the Sushruta Samhita with a full and comprehensive introduction*, additional texts, different readings, notes, comparative views, index, glossary and plates (Vol. 2), Published by the Author, Calcutta, 1911.

Bhishagratna, K.L. (Ed.), *An English translation of the Sushruta Samhita with a full and comprehensive introduction*, additional texts, different readings, notes, comparative views, index, glossary and plates (Vol. 3), S. L. Bhaduri, Calcutta, 1916.

VRIKSHA AYURVEDA

Sircar, N.N. and Sircar, Roma (eds), '*Vrksayurveda - A Treatise on Plant Science: Indian Medical Science Series No.38*', Sri Satguru Publications, a division of Indian Books Centre, New Delhi, 1996.

Rao, S.K. Ramachandra (ed), '*Vrukshayurveda - Excerpt from Sarngadhara Samhita*', Kalpatharu Research Academy, Bangalore, 1993.

IMAGE COPYRIGHT INFORMATION

RAISING READERS

Books Build Bright Futures

Dear Reader,

We hope you enjoyed reading this book and we'd love your attention for one more page, to share with you what's going on with children and books.

The number of children reading in their leisure time and for fun is in rapid decline. Young people have a lot of competition for their time, and a worryingly high number have only a few or no books at home.

If this is not a crisis already, it soon will be.

Studies have shown that reading for fun is the **single biggest predictor of a child's future success** – more than family circumstance, parents' educational background or income. It improves academic results, mental health, wealth, communication skills and ambition.

Our business works committedly to create books that are well-researched, engaging, and enduring, but here are some ways we can all raise more readers:

- Reading to children for just 10 minutes a day makes a difference
- Don't give up if children aren't regular readers – it's not just about the number of books they have or read but about encouraging interest and engagement
- Encourage them to listen to audiobooks
- Support schools and other libraries
- Give books as gifts

Thank you for reading: there's a lot more information about how to encourage children to read on our website.